Waterford

The Untaken City

Emmet Tobin

ISBN-13: 978-1545191606

ISBN-10: 1545191603

A Brief History

Waterford, Irelands oldest and the fifth most populous city in the Republic of Ireland at approximately 55,000 inhabitants.

The name 'Waterford' comes from Old Norse Veðrafjǫrðr. The Irish name is Port Láirge, meaning "Lárag's port".

Viking raiders first established a settlement near Waterford in 853. It and all the other longphorts were vacated in 902, the Vikings having been driven out by the native Irish. The Vikings re-established themselves in Ireland at Waterford in 914, led at first by Ottir Iarla (Jarl Ottar) until 917, and after that by Ragnall ua Ímair and the Uí Ímair dynasty, and built what would be Ireland's first city. Among the most prominent rulers of Waterford was Ivar of Waterford.

In 1167, Diarmait Mac Murchada, the deposed King of Leinster, failed in an attempt to take Waterford. He returned in 1170 with Cambro-Norman mercenaries under Richard de Clare, 2nd Earl of Pembroke (known as Strongbow); together they besieged and took the city after a desperate defence. In furtherance of the Norman invasion of Ireland, King Henry II of England landed at Waterford in 1171. Waterford and then Dublin were declared royal cities, with Dublin also declared capital of Ireland.

Waterford is the main city of Ireland's South-East Region. Historically Waterford was an important trading port which brought much prosperity to the city throughout the city's eventful history.

Waterford Port is Ireland's closest deep-water port to mainland Europe, handling approximately 12% of Ireland's external trade by value. Waterford is the site of a number of multinationals with many companies within the life science industry represented locally.

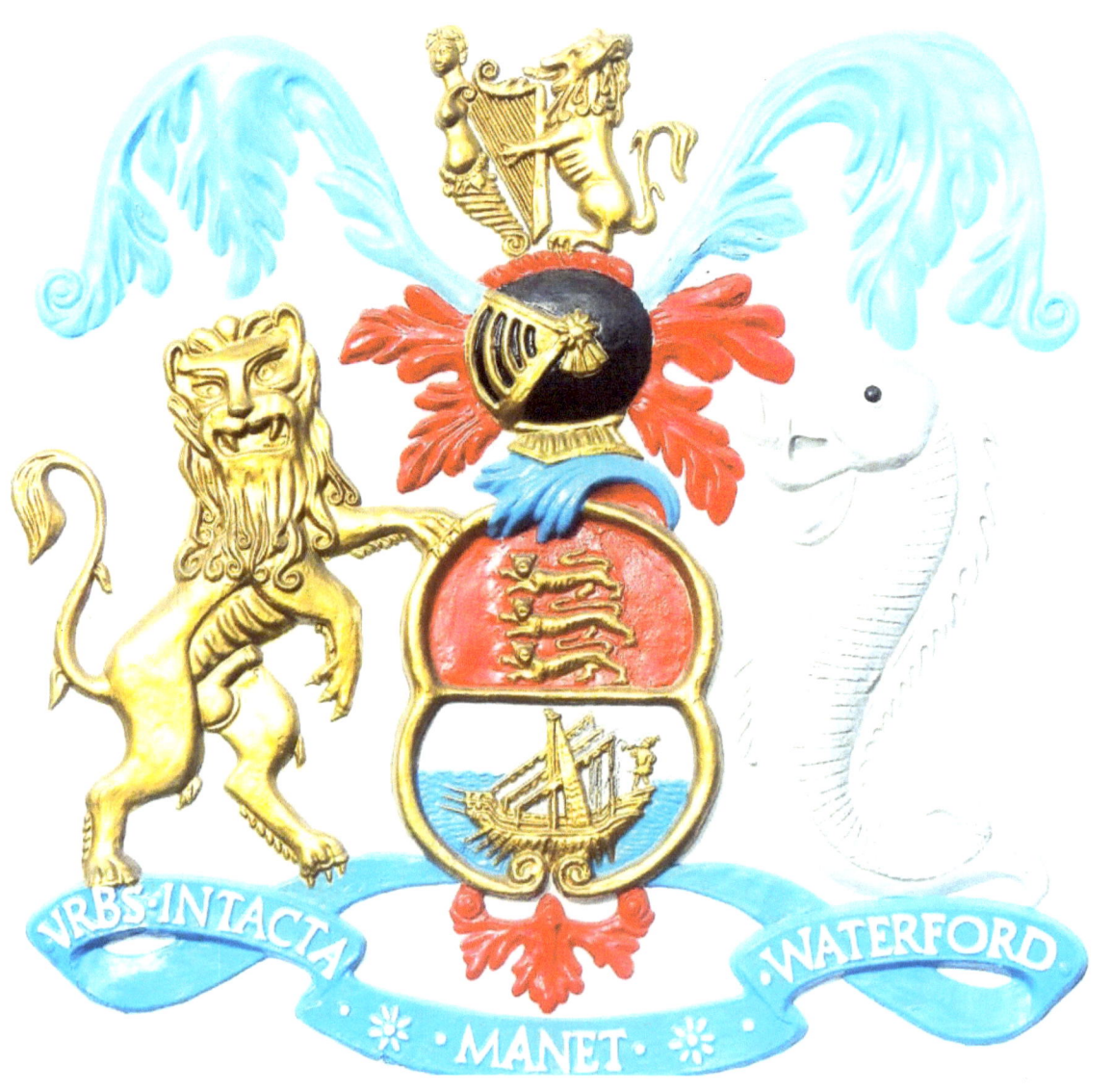

Urbs Intacta Manet Waterford

Special thanks to:

Bee Leavy

and

Craig Butler

for their input and making this work possible.

Contents

Waterford –The Untaken City

Waterford –The Untaken City

Opposite (Top): Waterford Distillery, located on the banks of the River Suir. Previously Diageo operated a Brewery at the site. The facility was converted into a distillery in 2015.

Opposite (Bottom): Pictured from Grattan Quay, Waterford City. The Edmund Rice Bridge can be seen at high time.

Below (this page): The control tower at Plunkett station, Waterford City.

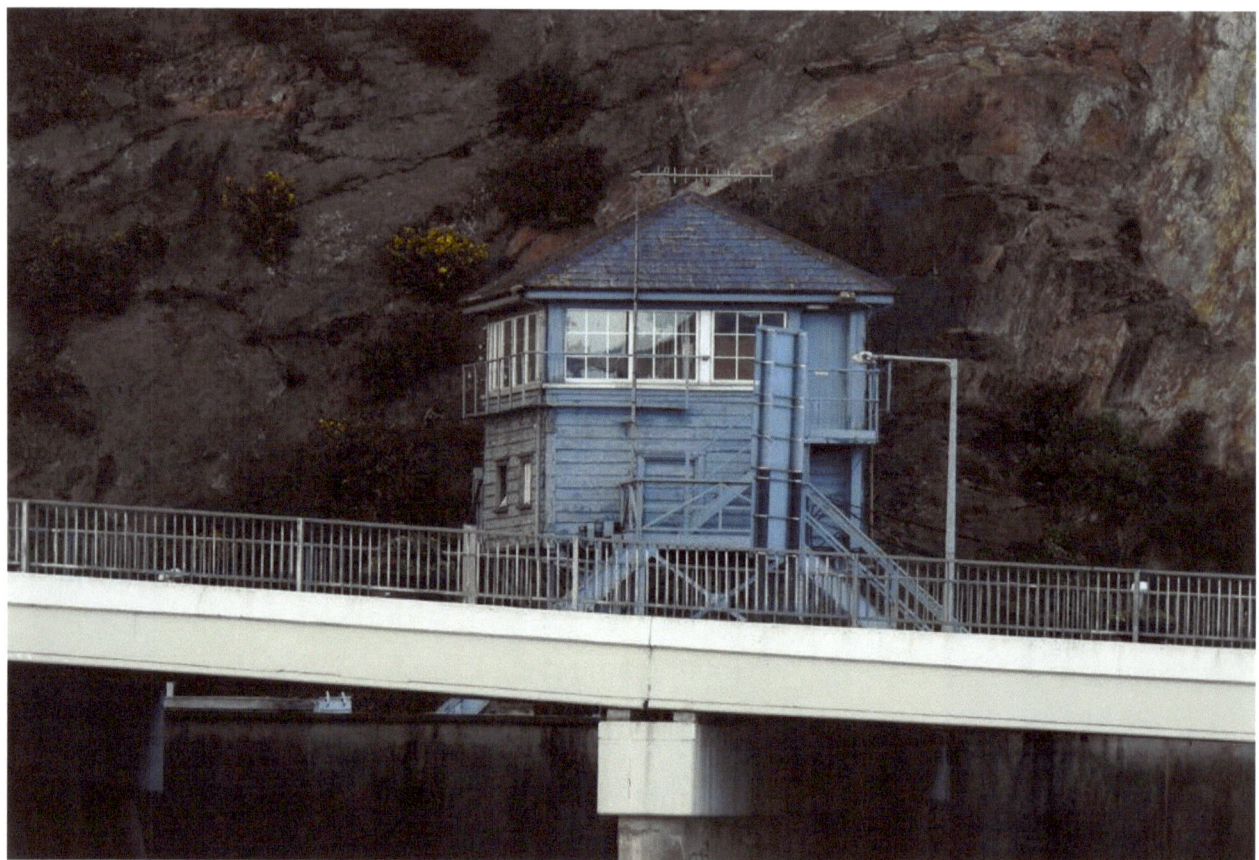

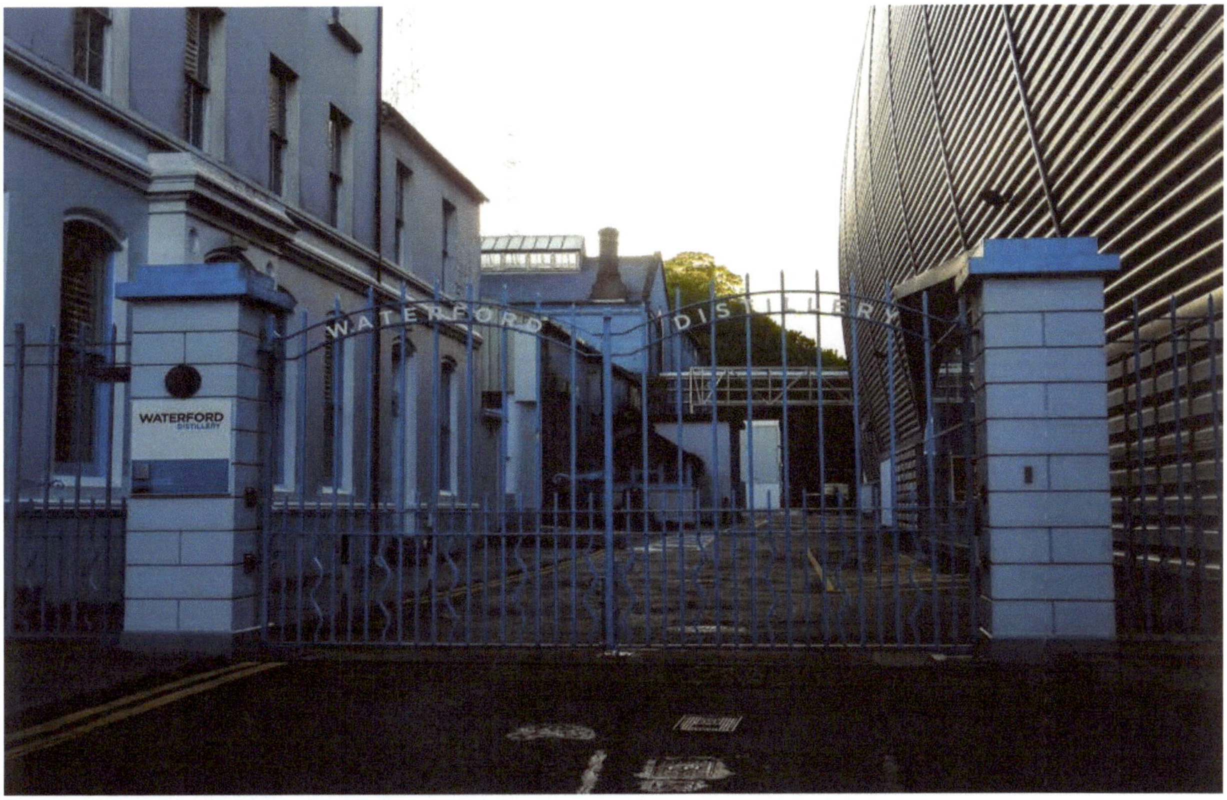
WATERFORD DISTILLERY
WATERFORD
DISTILLERY

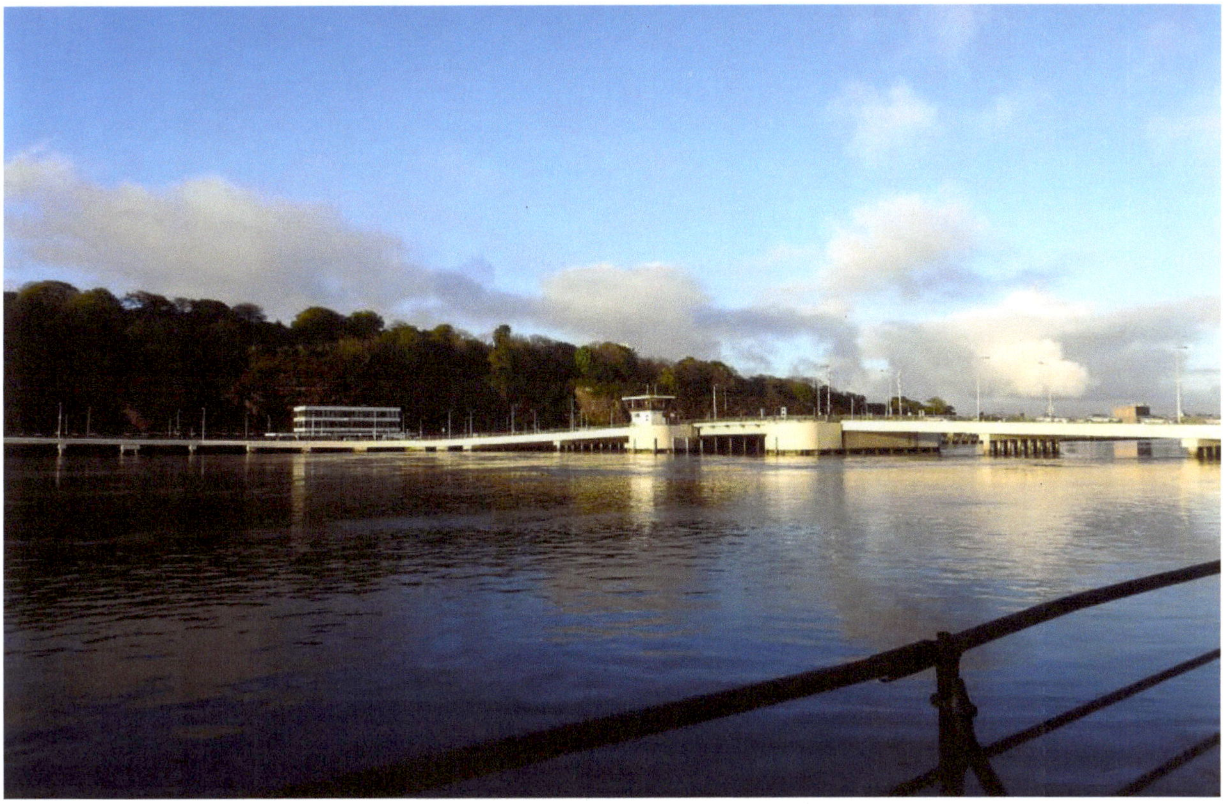

Opposite: Along the North Quay, the Merchant Thug, (MT) Tramontane is moored. Powered by two Crepelle engines that produce 2,500 brake horse power. Pictured on the city side is the MT Bargarth.

Below: The cable stayed bring spans the river Suir. At 230 metres, the main span has the longest single bridge span in the Republic of Ireland.

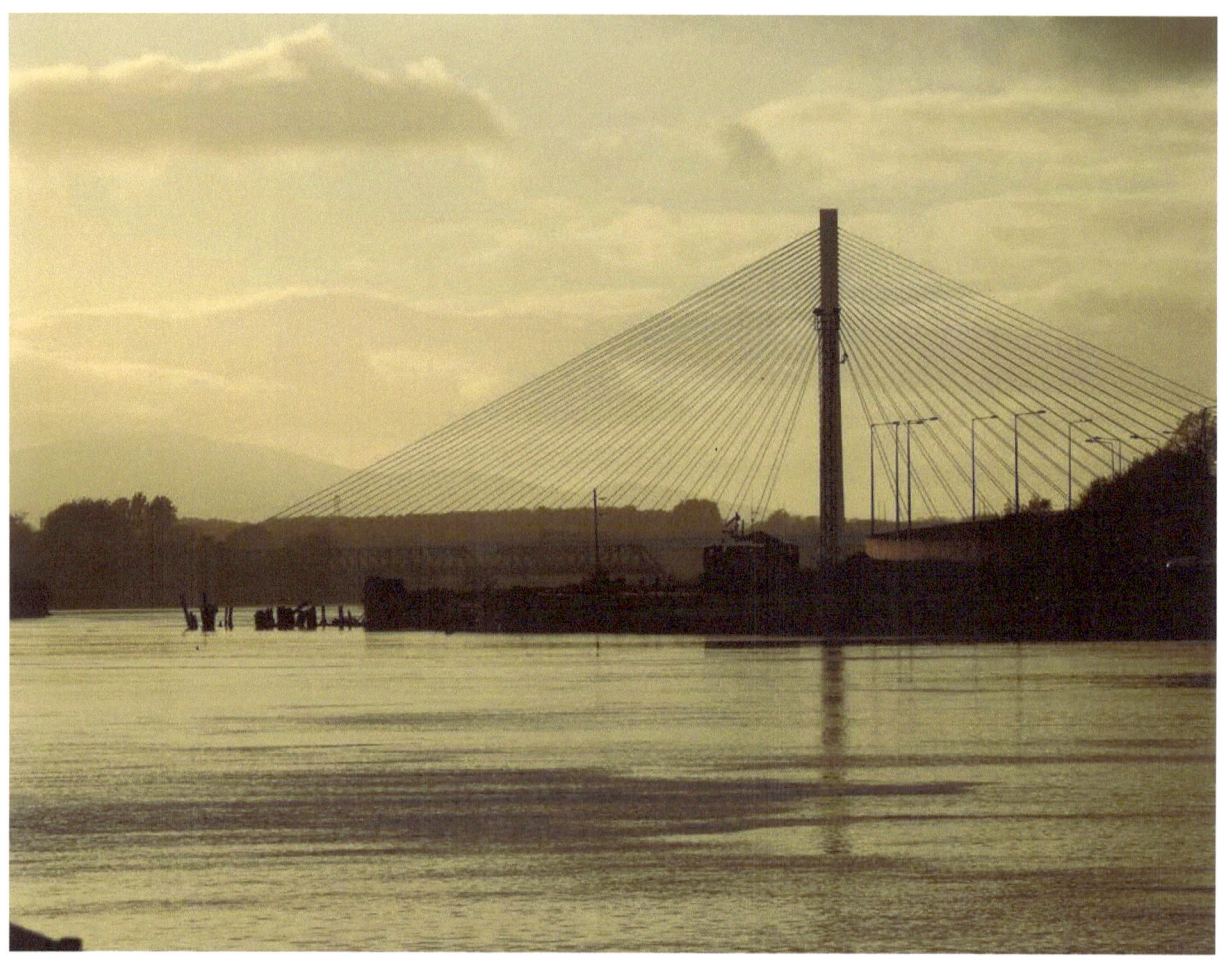

Waterford –The Untaken City

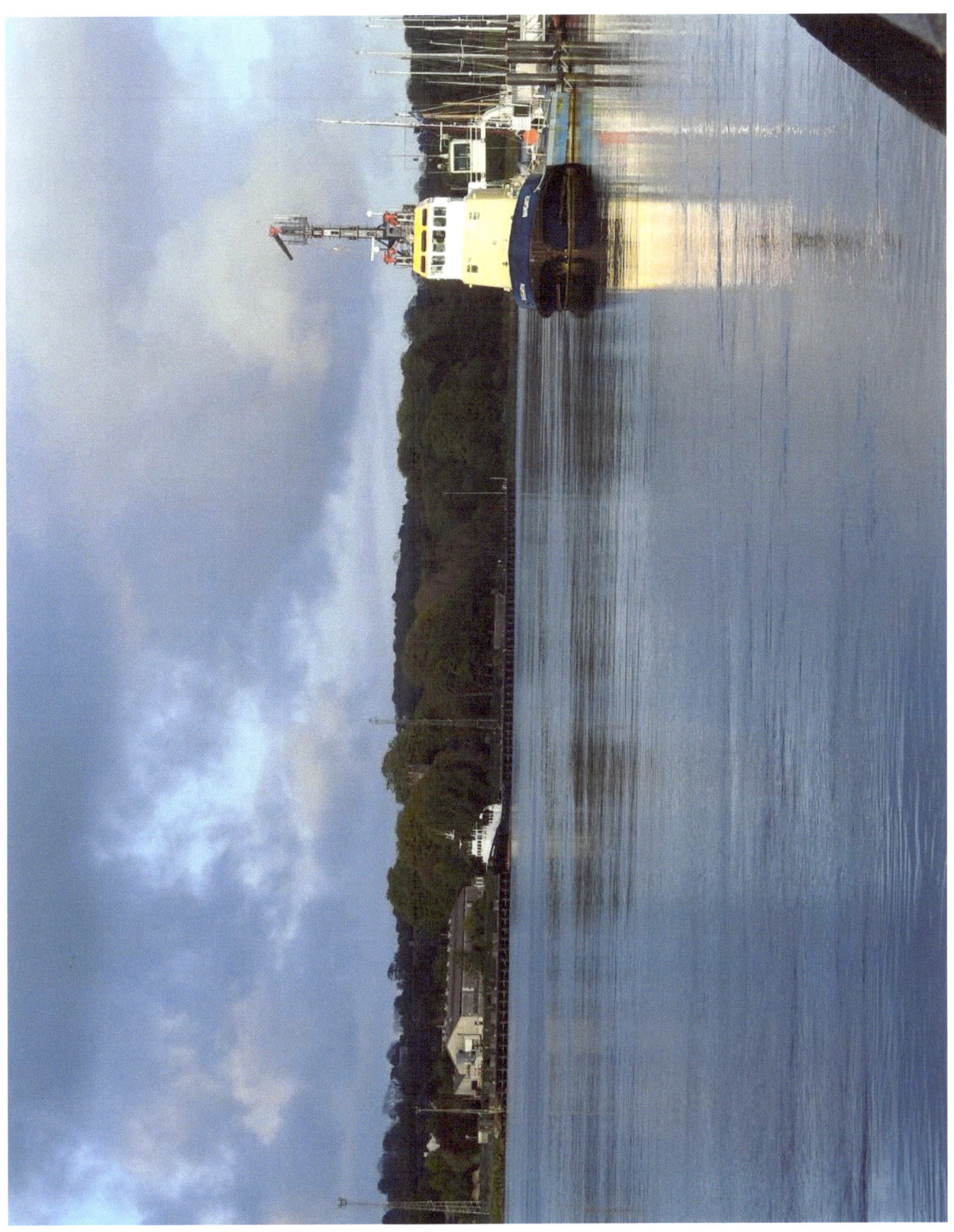

Opposite: The sculpture located at Grattan Quay, designed to celebrate the city's rich maritime and industrial history.

Below: Like a fish out of water, an old fishing boat lies dockside in Newrath, Co. Kilkenny.

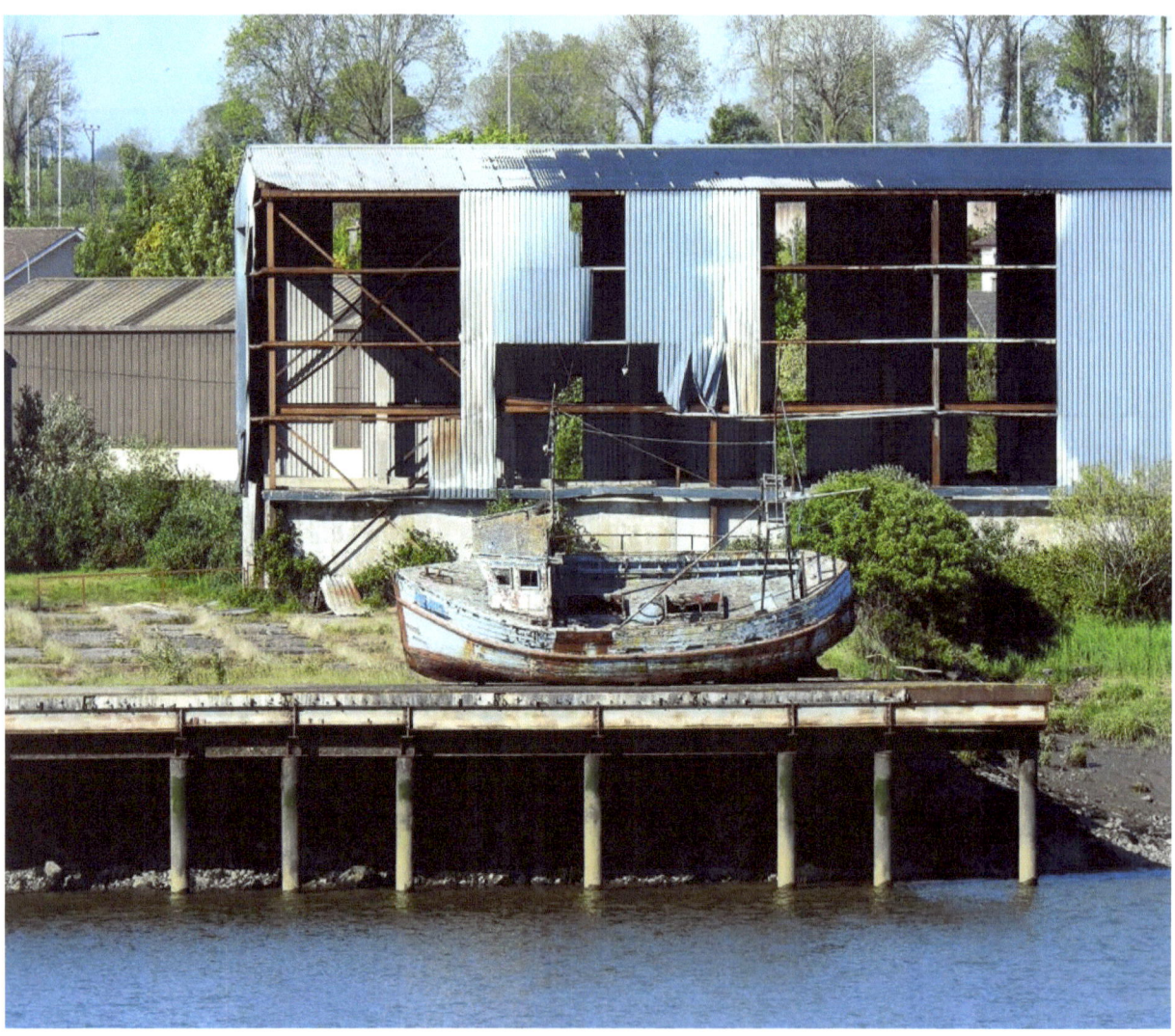

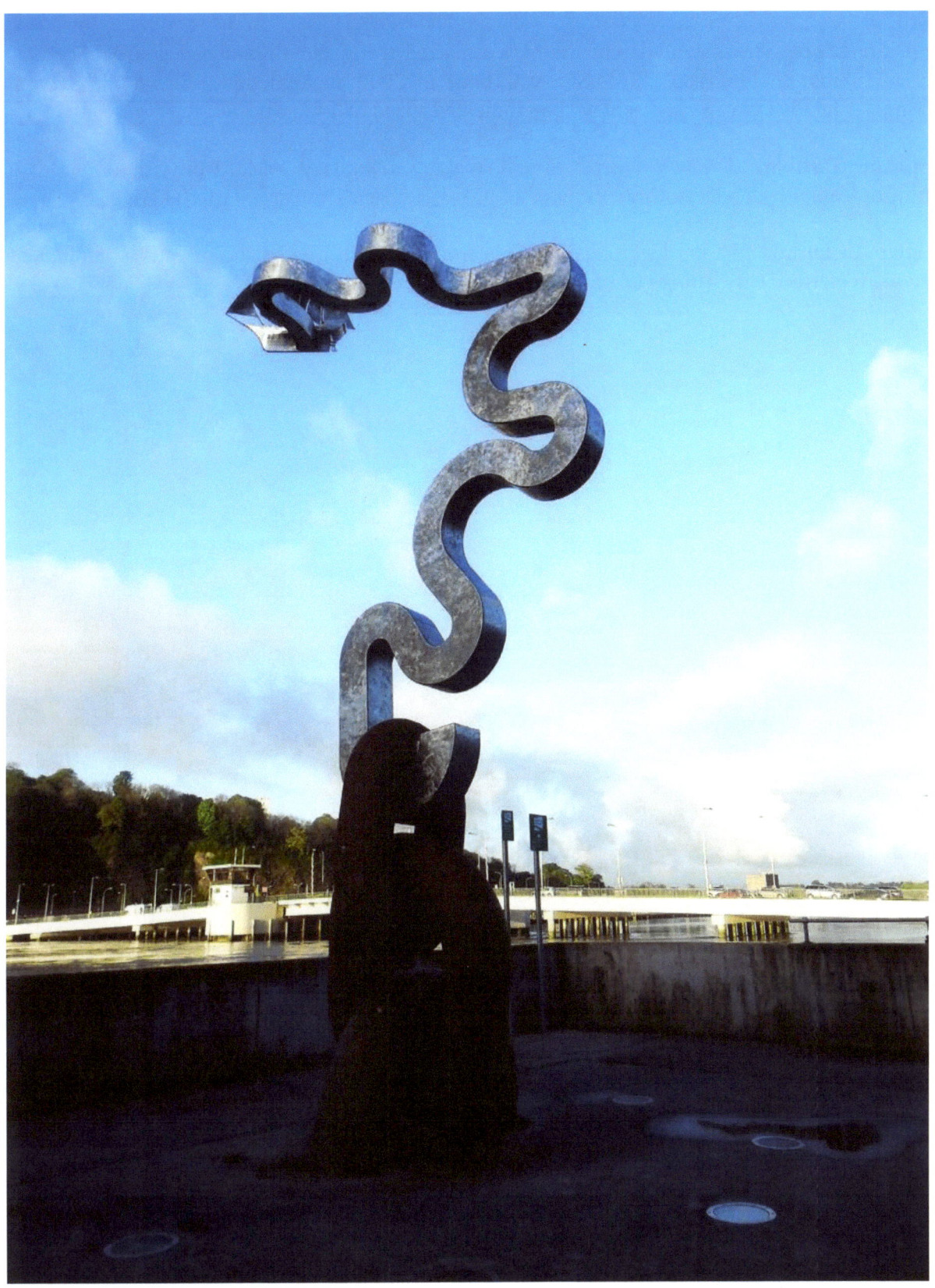

Opposite (Top): Stavros S. Niarchos is a two masted (brig) tall ship owned and operated by the Tall Ships Youth Trust (TSYT).She was built in 2000 at Appledore shipyard in Devon. During her maiden voyage, she achieved an indicated speed of 14 knots.

Opposite (Bottom): The MV Fastnet Sound, making towards Waterford city, described as a MultiCat Vessel with a Deck Crane situated onboard, it boasts a top speed of 10 knots.

Below: An Iarnród Éireann locomotive travels from Co. Wexford in the direction of Plunkett Station, Waterford City. (Photo taken from Kings Channel)

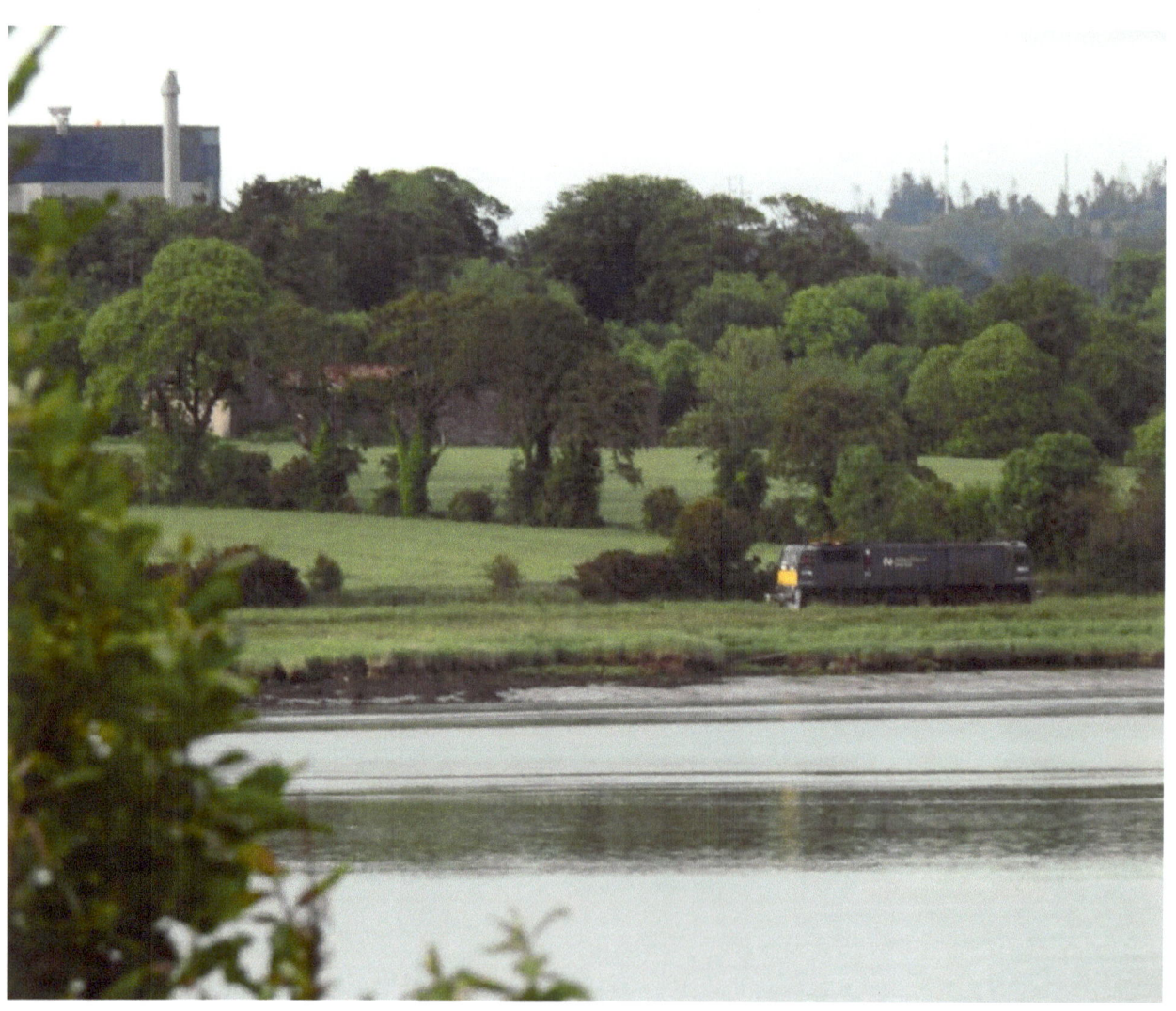

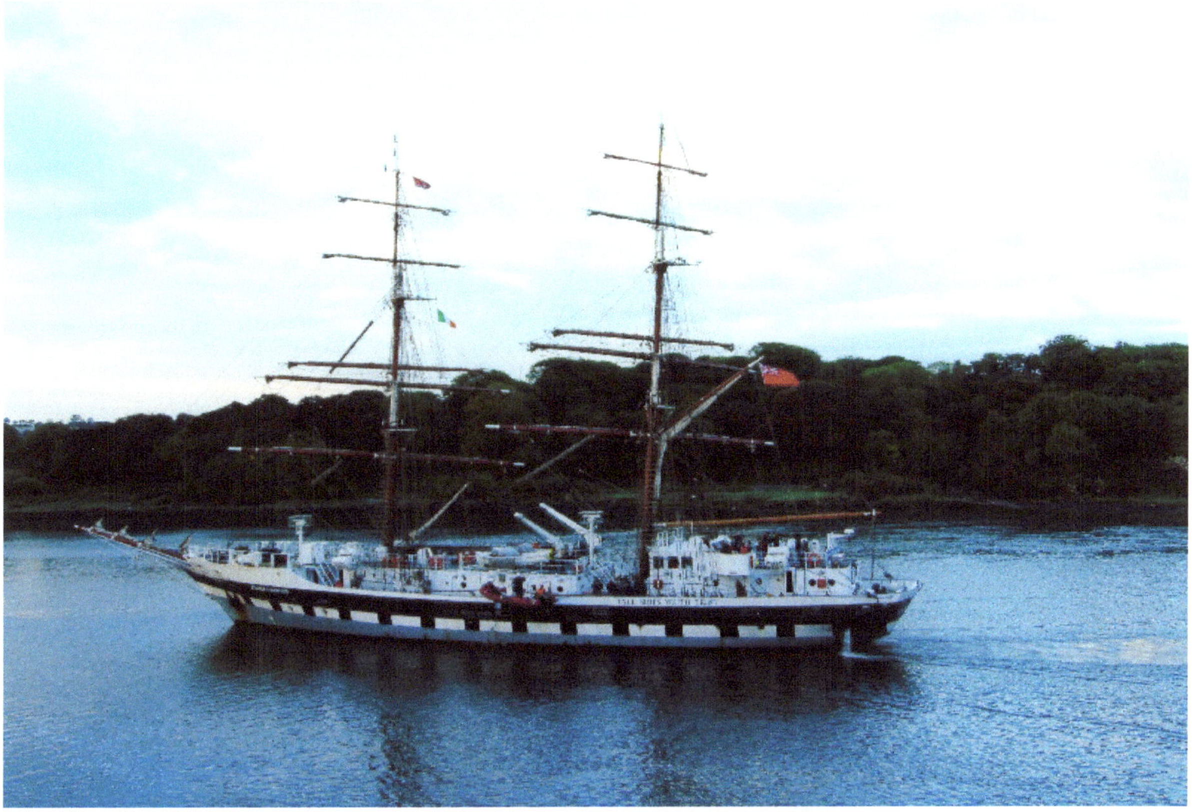

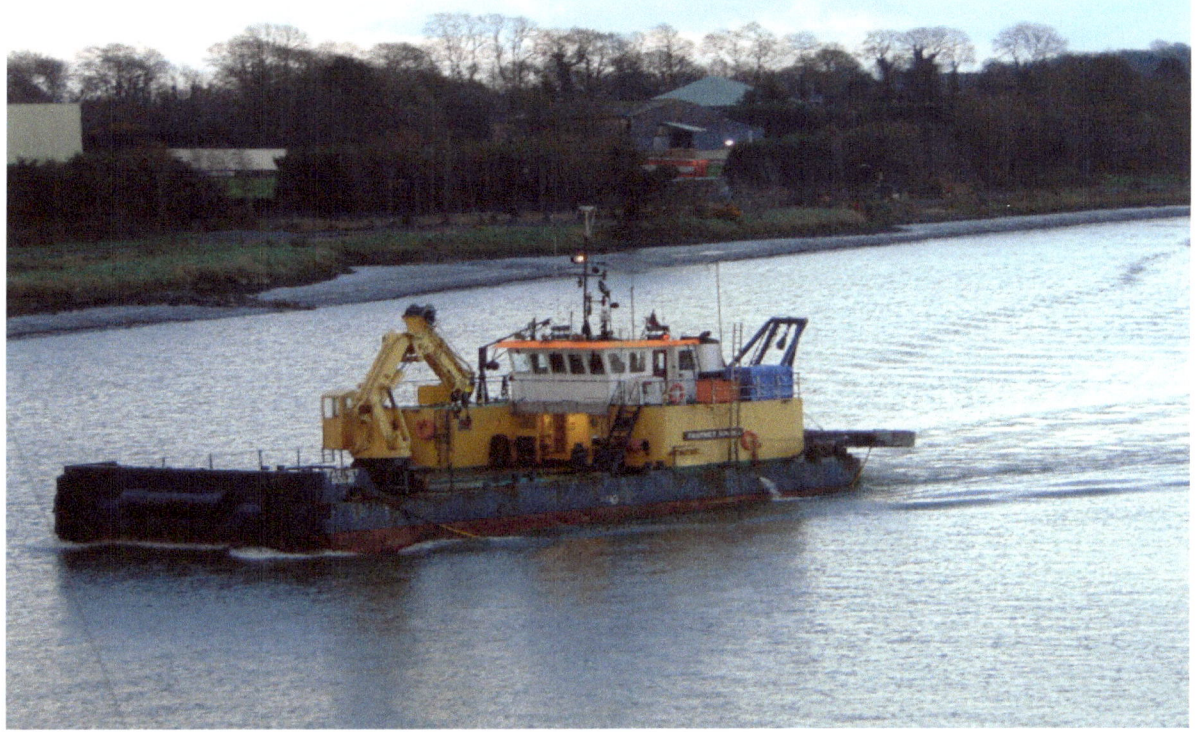

Opposite (Top): "Madigans", an Off license located in the heart of the town. Empty large stout glass bottles accepted.

Opposite (Bottom): The Kings Bar. Famous for hosting Sunday morning open mic sessions as an alternative to Morning Mass. The pub is now closed.

Below: Marine Bellafont, located on St. Johns River, in the vicinity of the Marine Hotel.

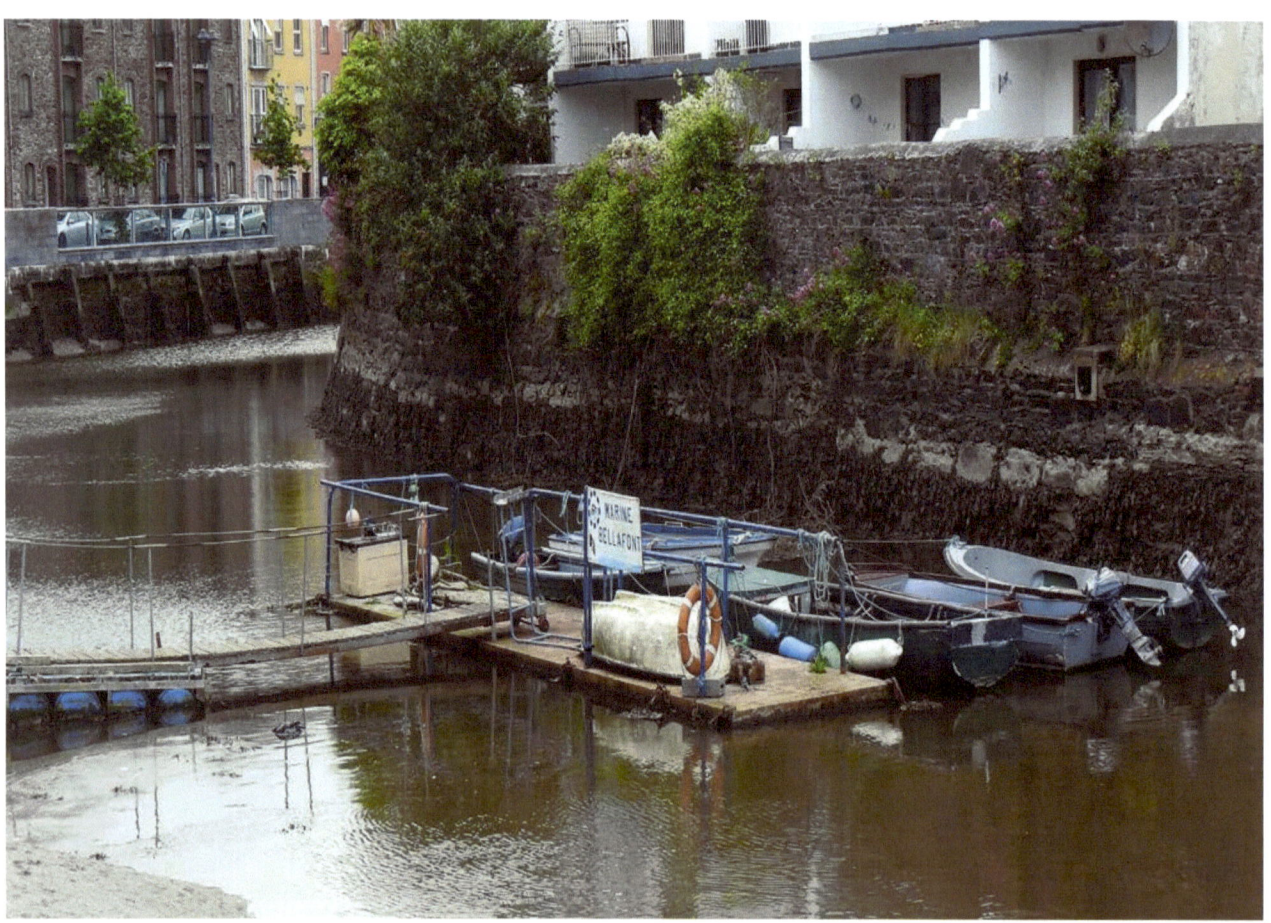

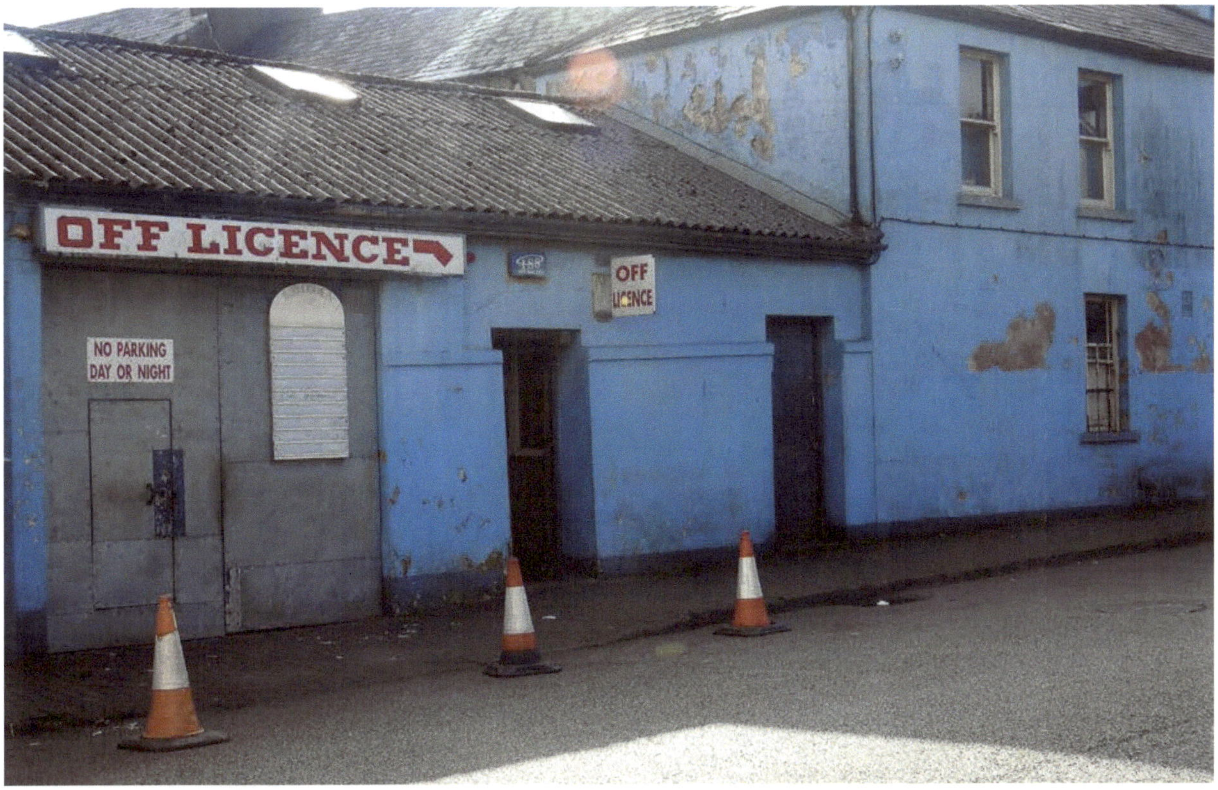
OFF LICENCE
NO PARKING
DAY OR NIGHT
OFF
LICENCE

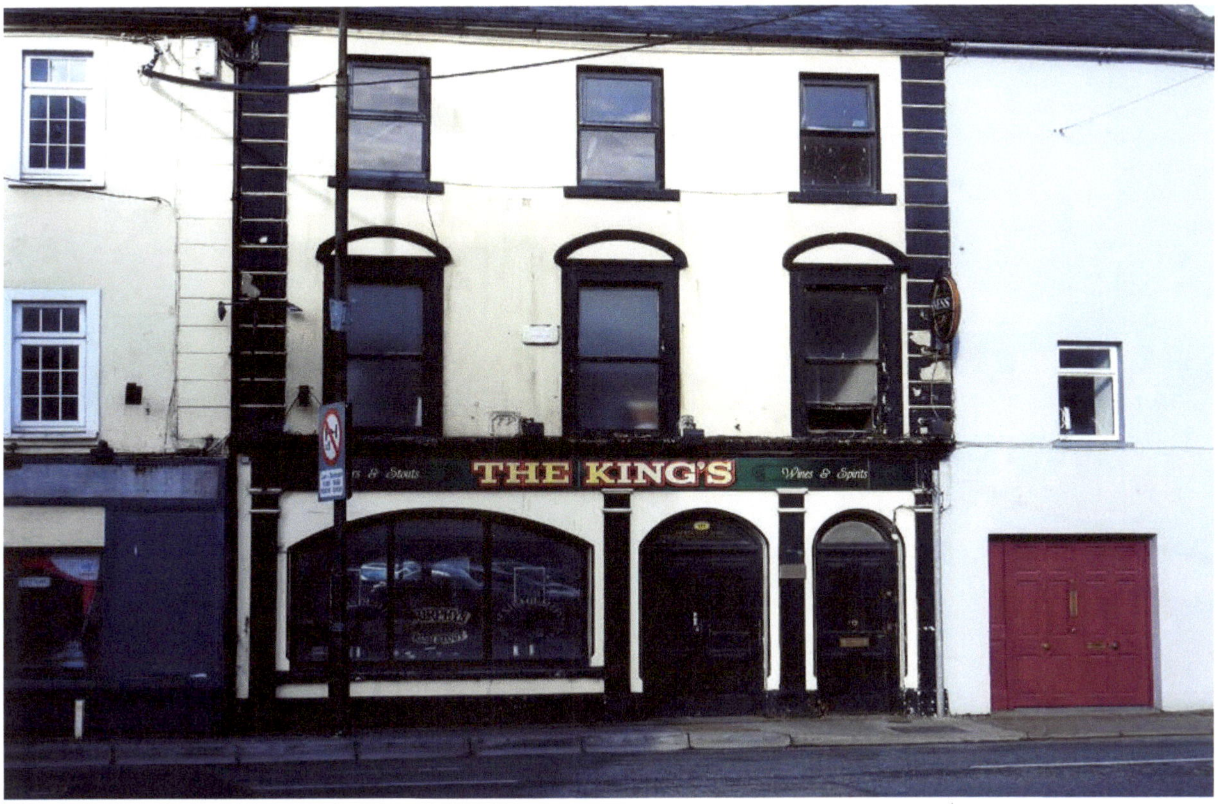
THE KING'S
Vines & Spirits

Opposite (Top): The Blessed Virgin Mary, St. Johns Park.

Opposite (Bottom): The Grotto at Belvedere built through the voluntary labour of Belvedere residents. Erected in 1981.

Below: The footbridge that adjoins Georges Quay and Adelphi Quay in the city.

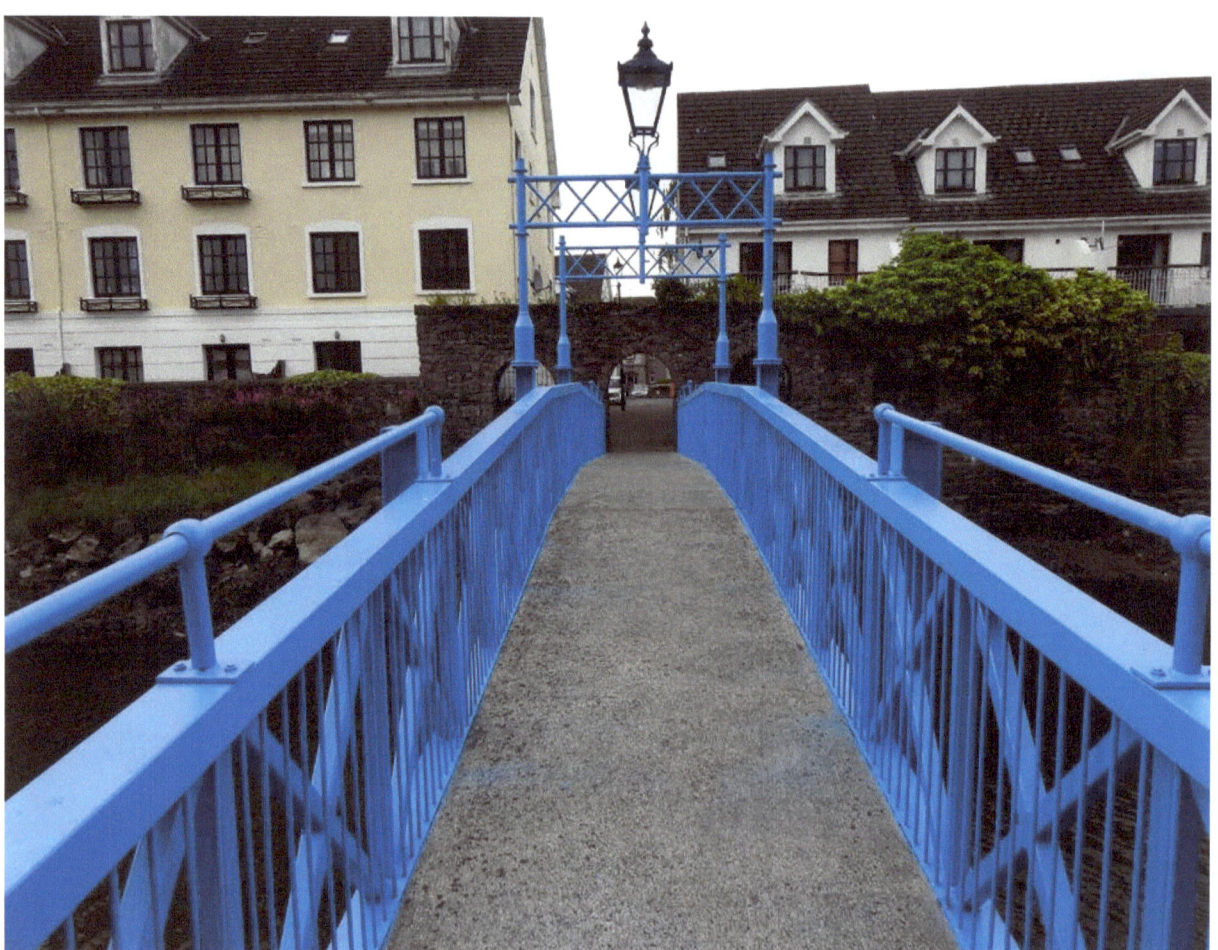

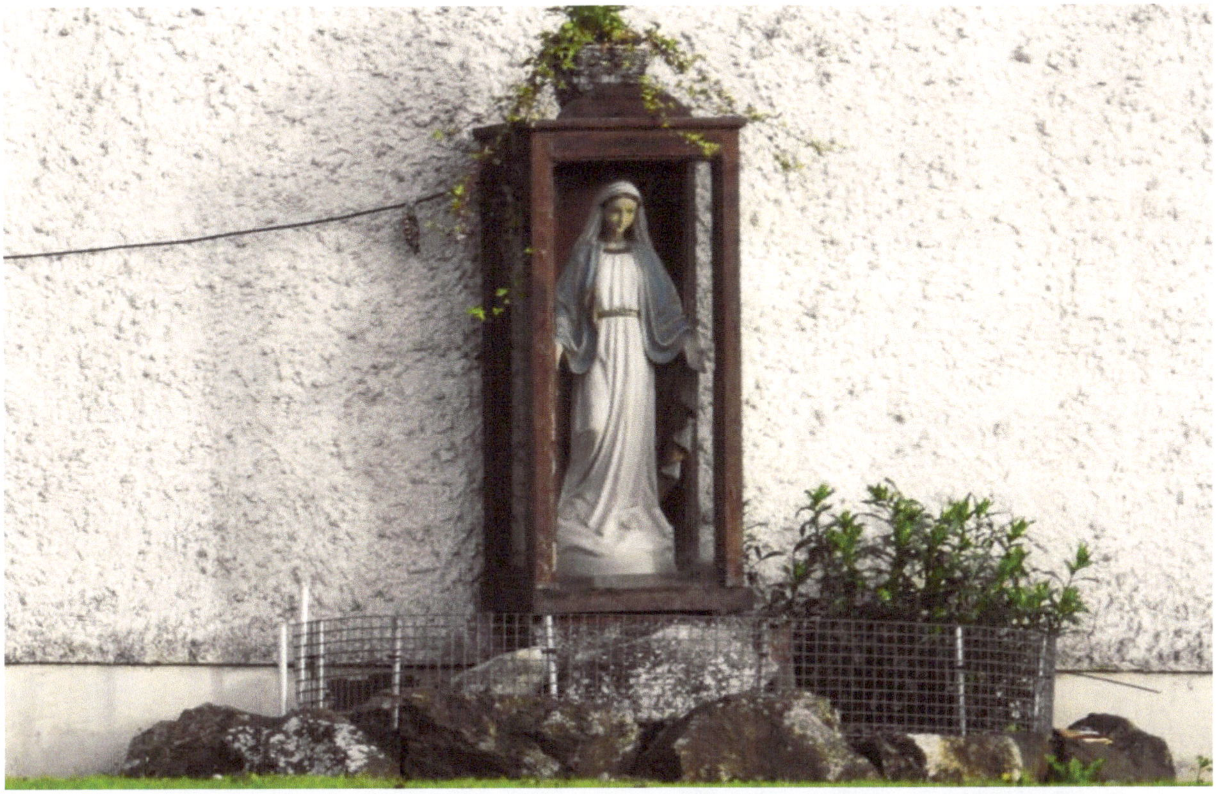

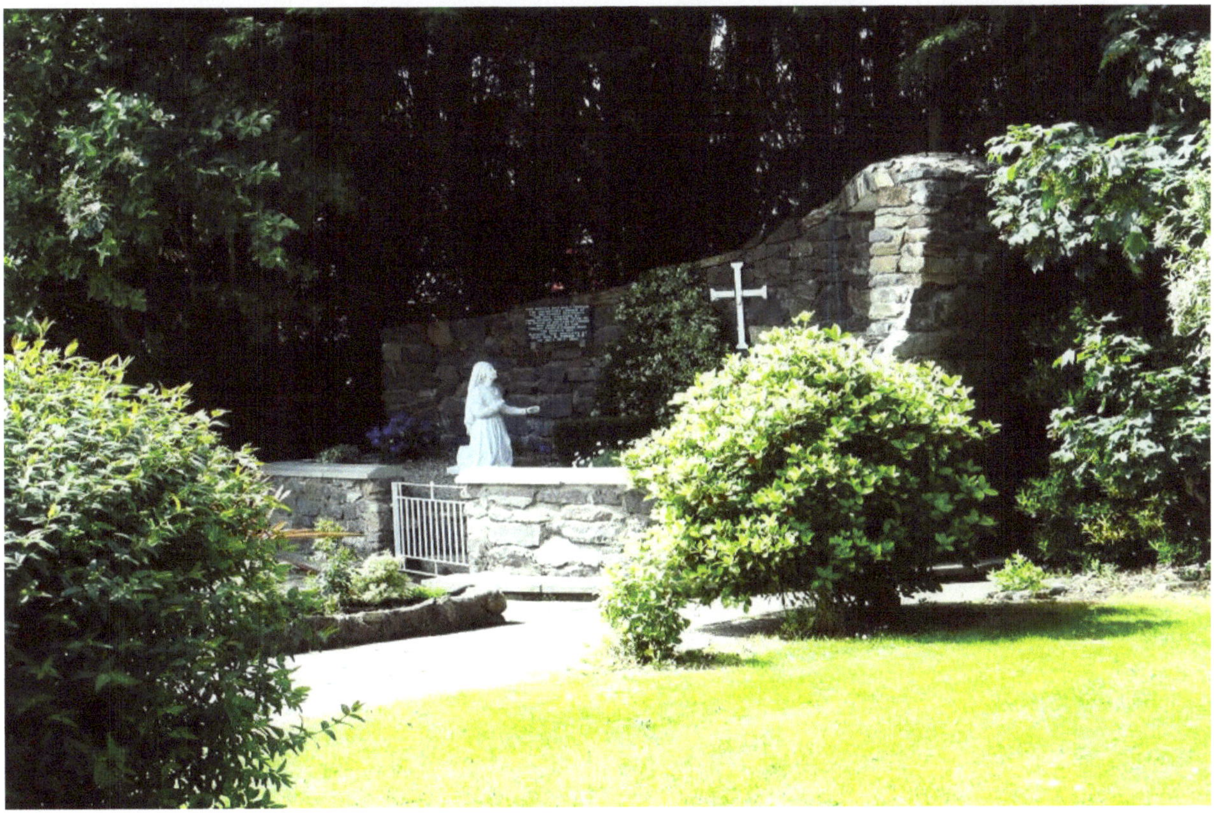

Opposite (Top): The now closed Maryland.

Opposite (Bottom): The Viking Triangle experience in Waterford City is decorated with miniature Bronze models representing the streets and landmarks within the city.

Below: The city walls close to Little Patricks Street Waterford City.

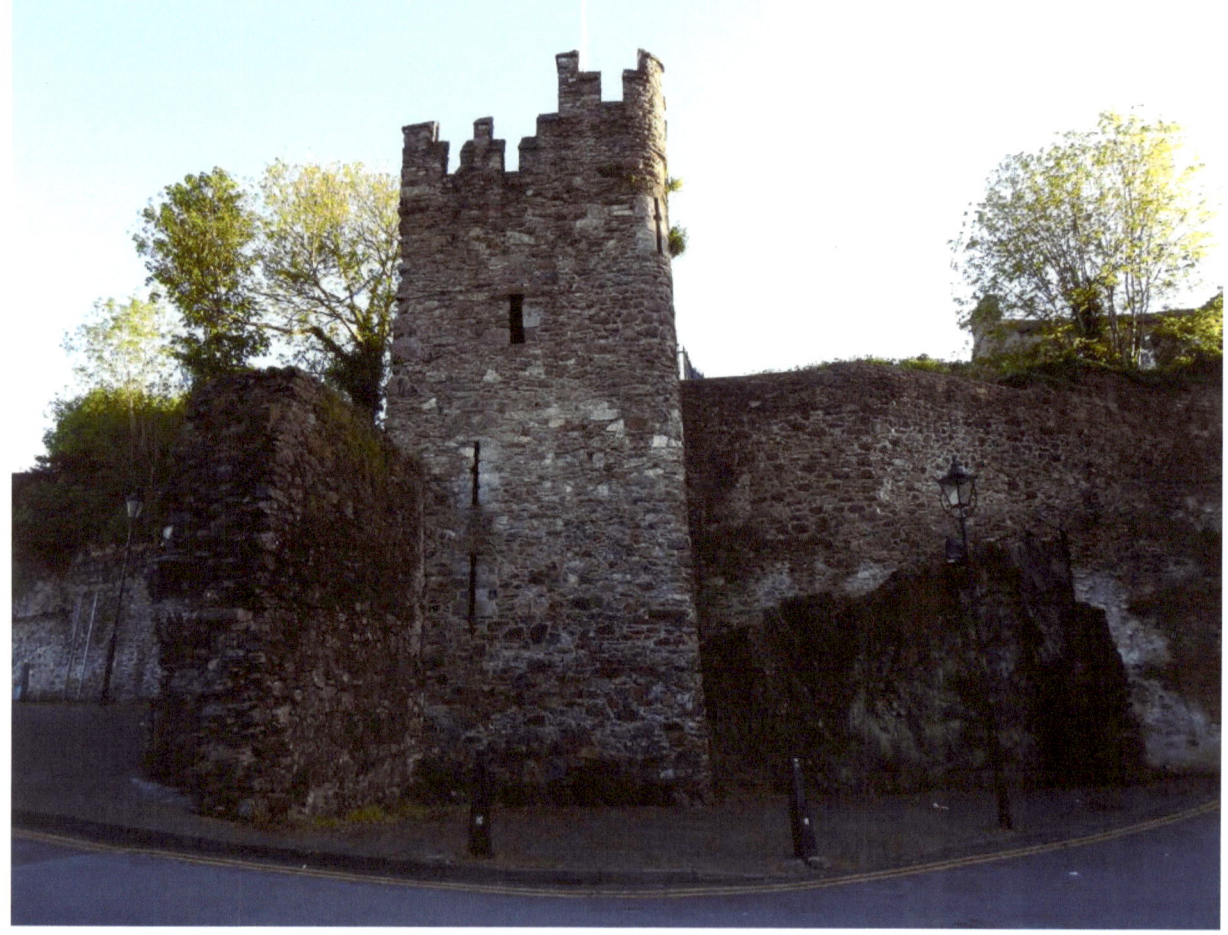

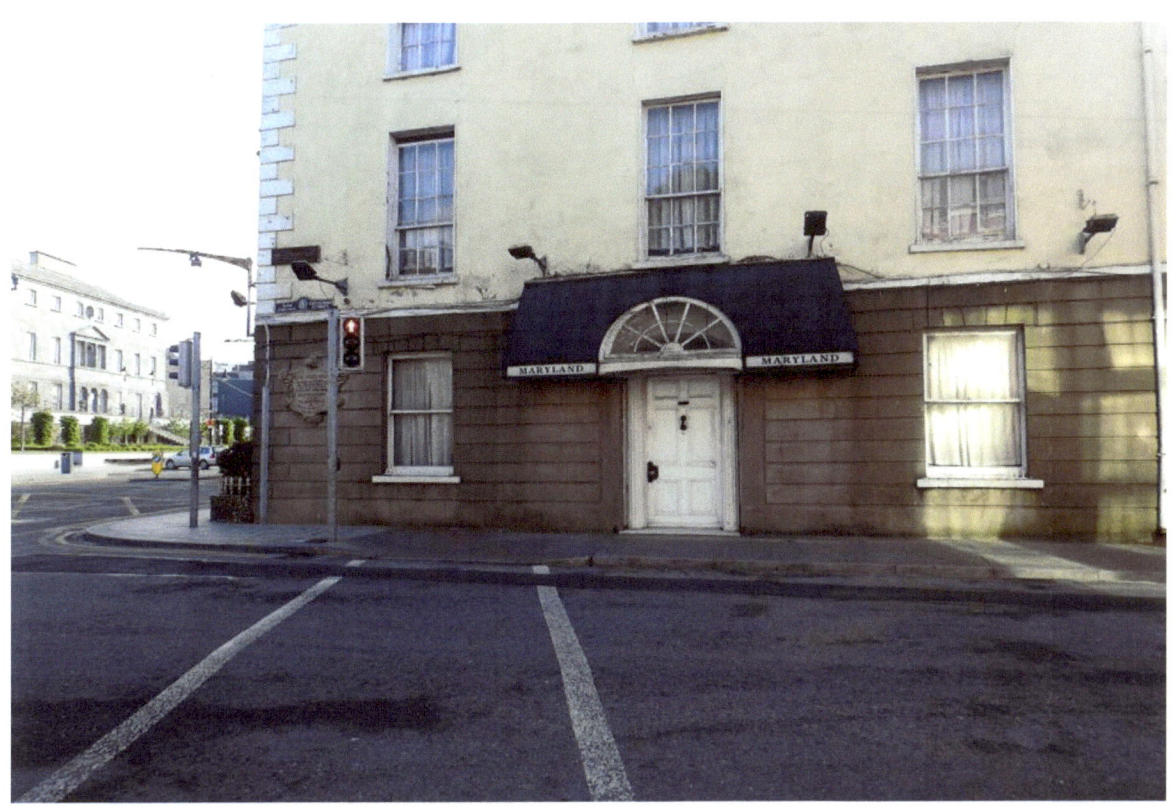

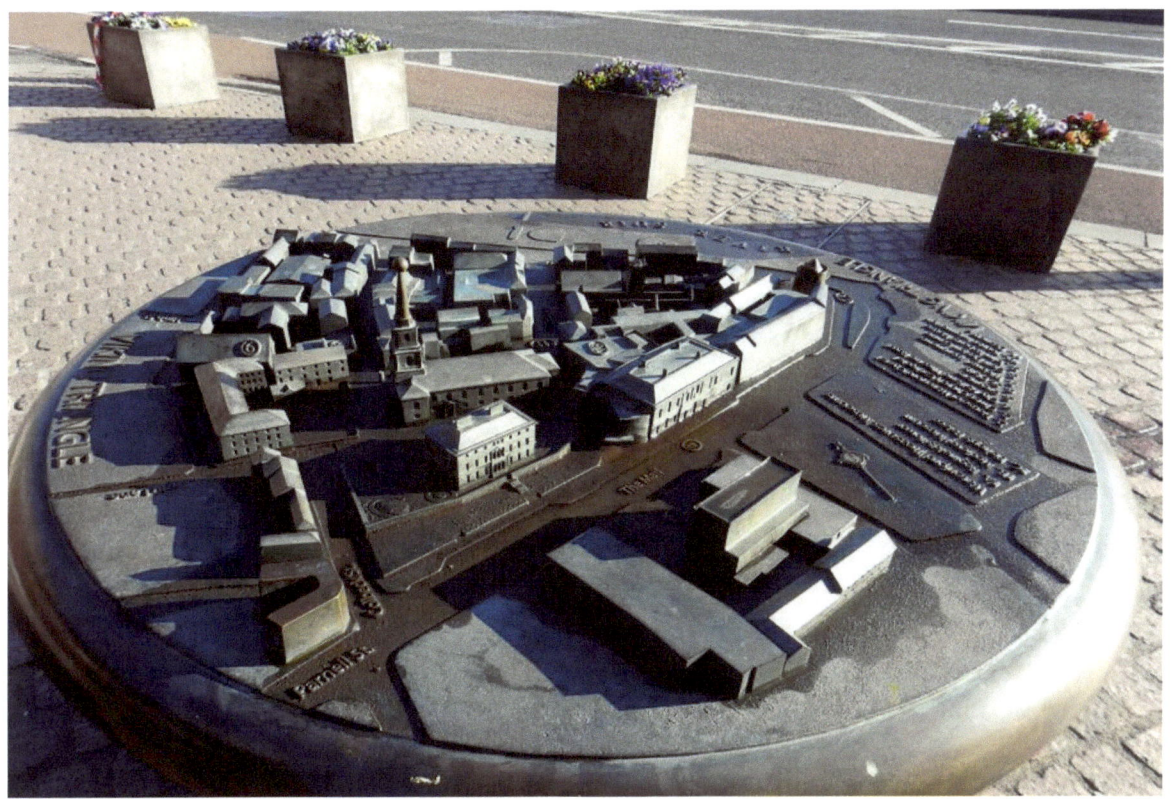

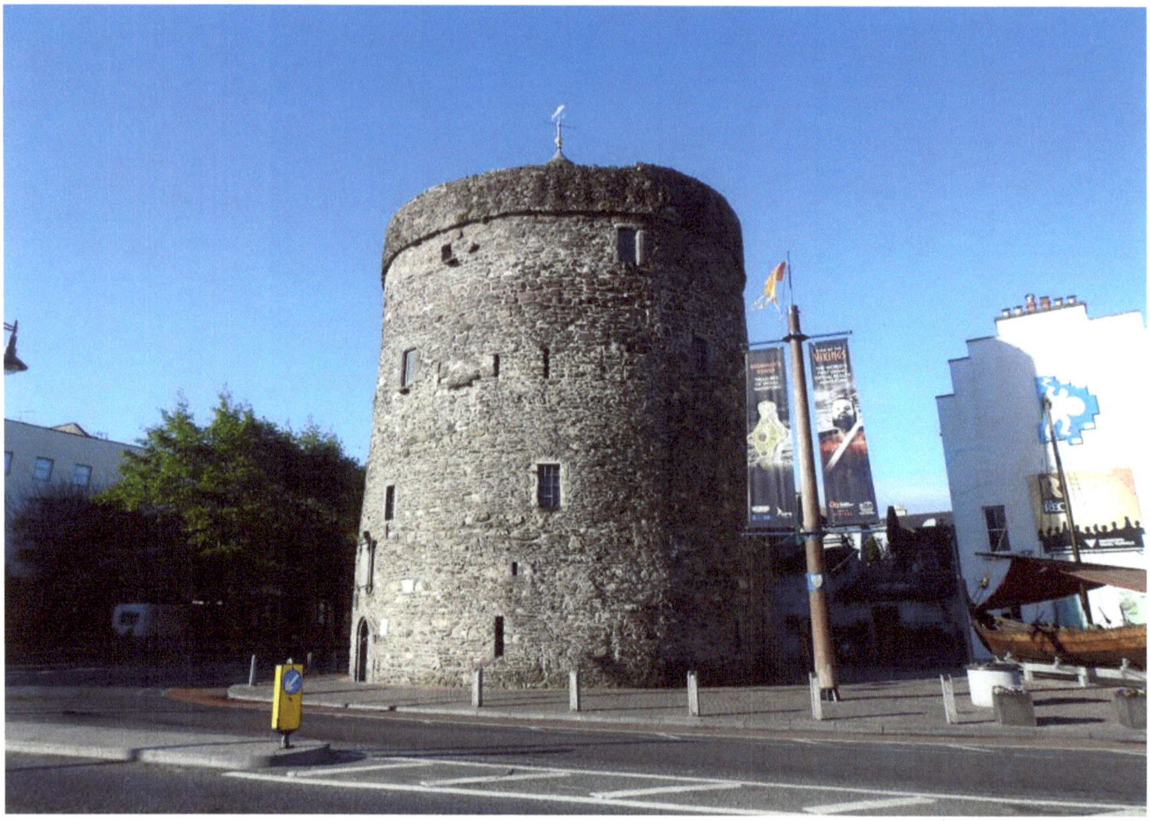

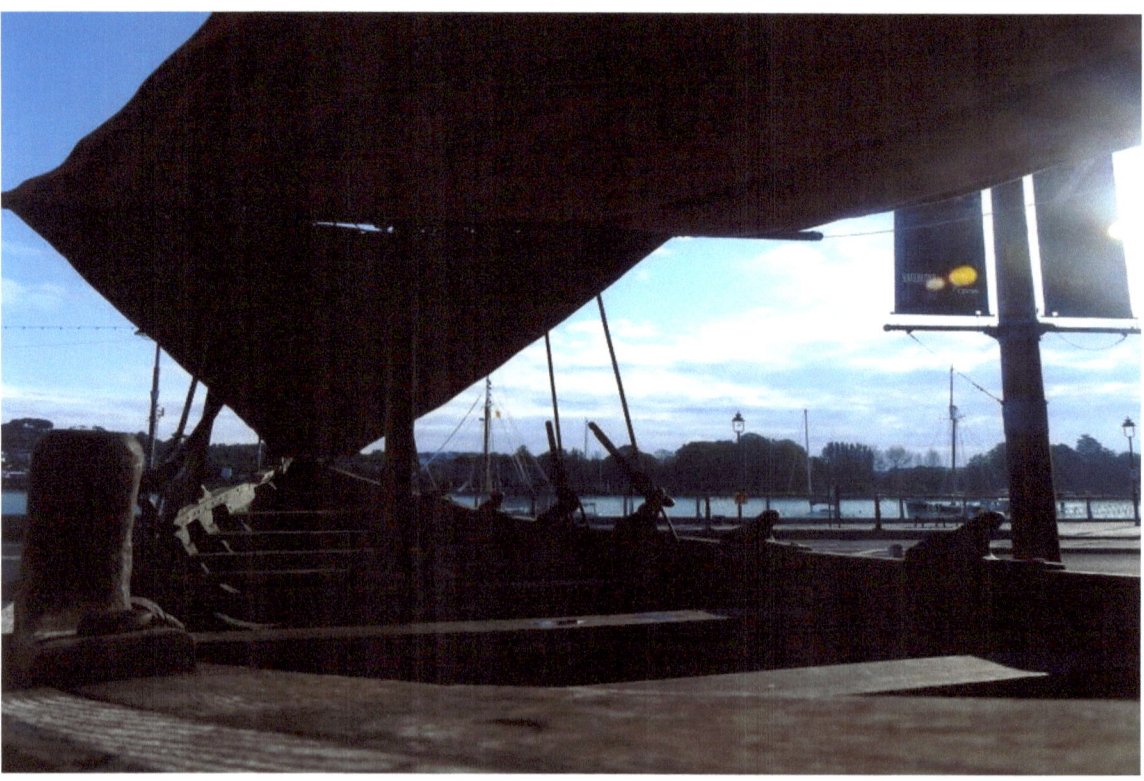

Opposite Page (Top): Reginalds Tower, The tower's name seems to refer to one of the many Viking rulers of the town that bore the name. One possibility is that it refers to Ragnall mac Gillemaire, the last Hiberno-Norse ruler of the town The present tower is likely to have been built in the 13th or 14th century; it may have been constructed between 1253 and 1280

In 1649, Waterford was besieged by the army of the English parliamentarian Oliver Cromwell, but he failed to capture the city on that occasion. They returned in 1650, and this time they were successful. A cannonball, visible high up the wall on the north side of the building, is lodged firmly in the wall, and is reputed to be from this siege.

In 1690, following his defeat at the Battle of the Boyne, James II of England is said to have climbed to the top of the tower to take a last look at his lost kingdom before embarking for exile in France. During the 17th and 18th centuries, the tower was used to store munitions. In the early 19th century it functioned as a prison.

Opposite (Bottom): Located beside Reginald's Tower. This replica long boat vessel is 12 metres (39 feet) in length. It was built by a local shipwright and sailed locally before going to its present exhibition space on Parade Quay. In the background, the River Suir can be seen.

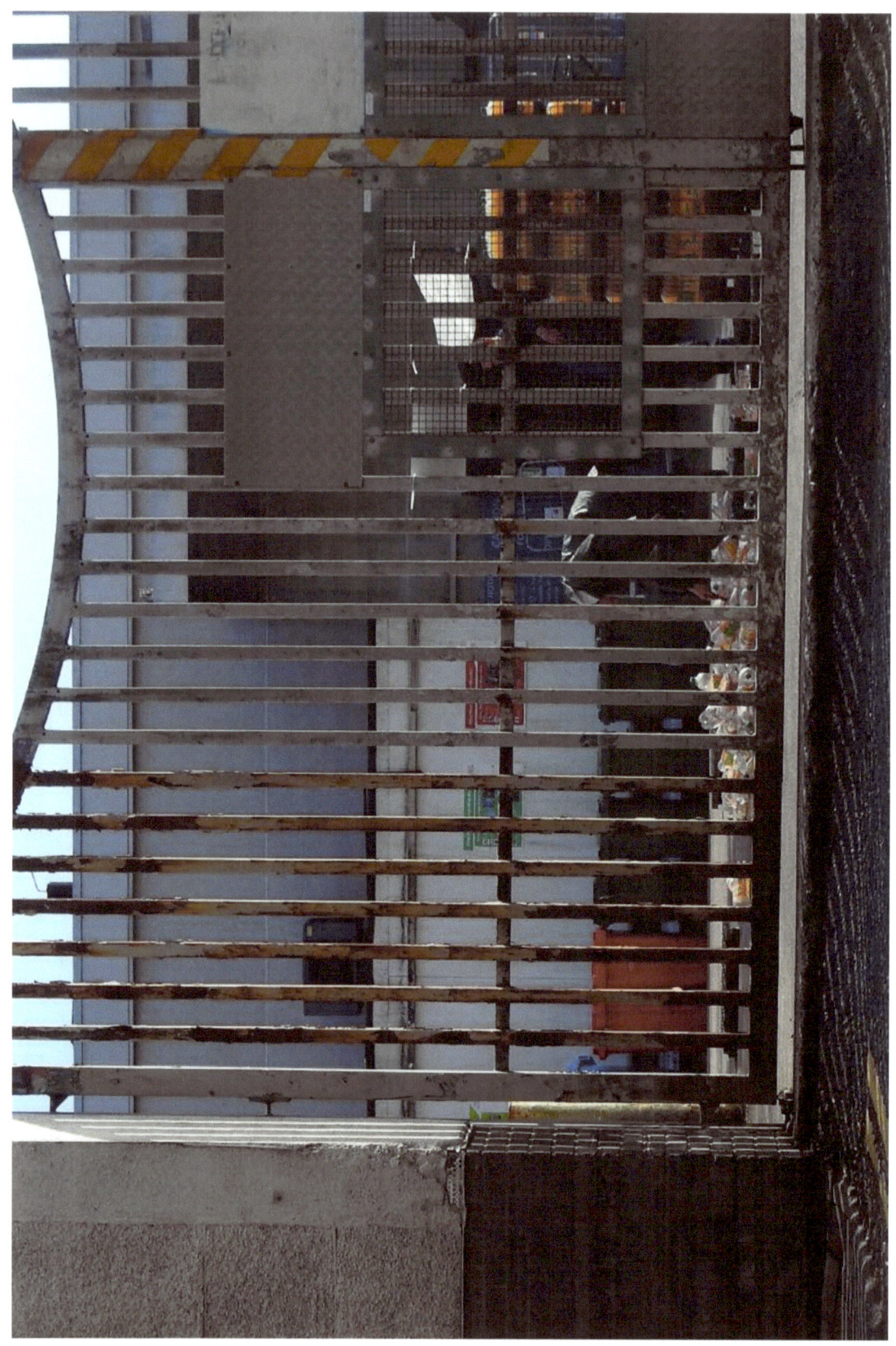

Opposite: Orange Squash

Below: The now closed Strand Electric. Once, one of the few electrical goods providers in the city.

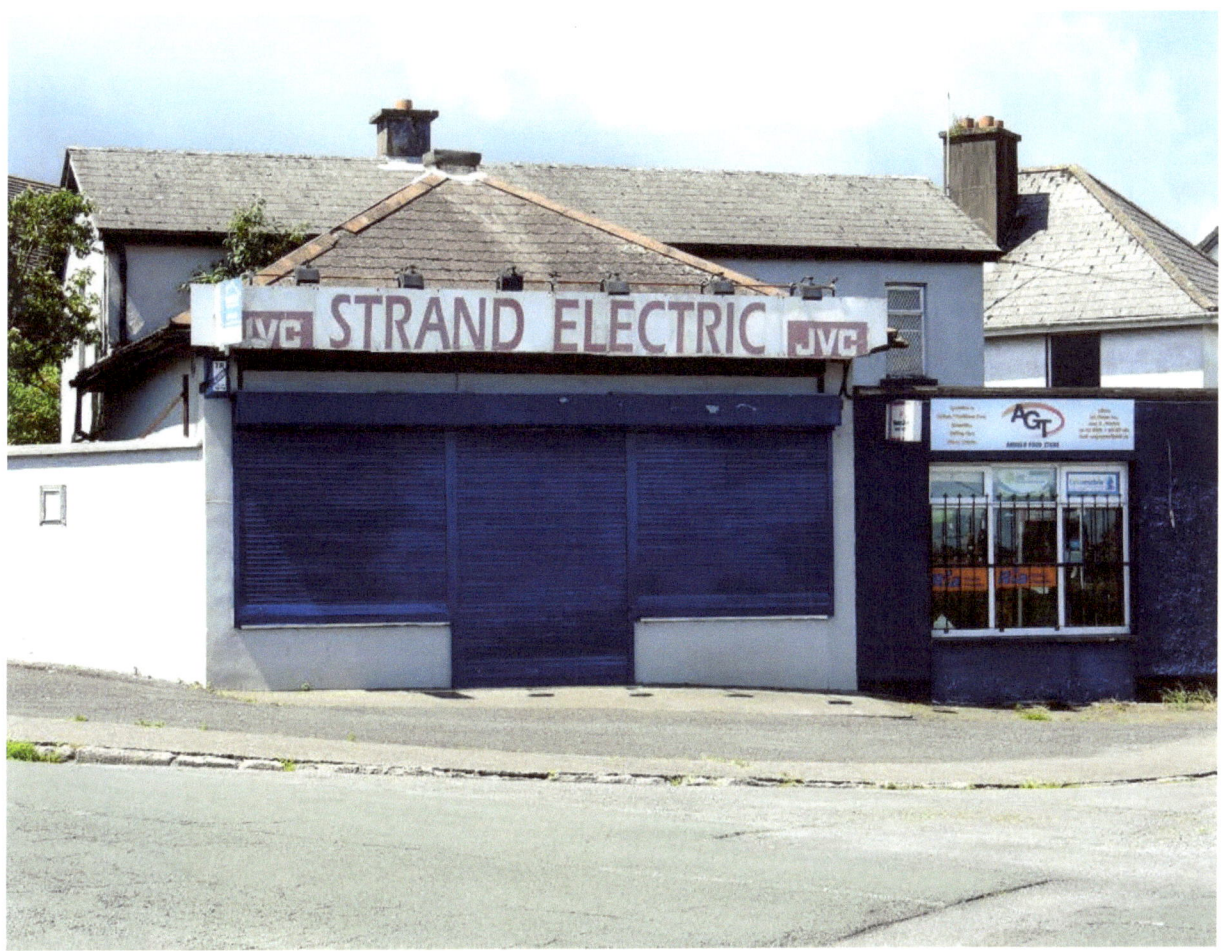

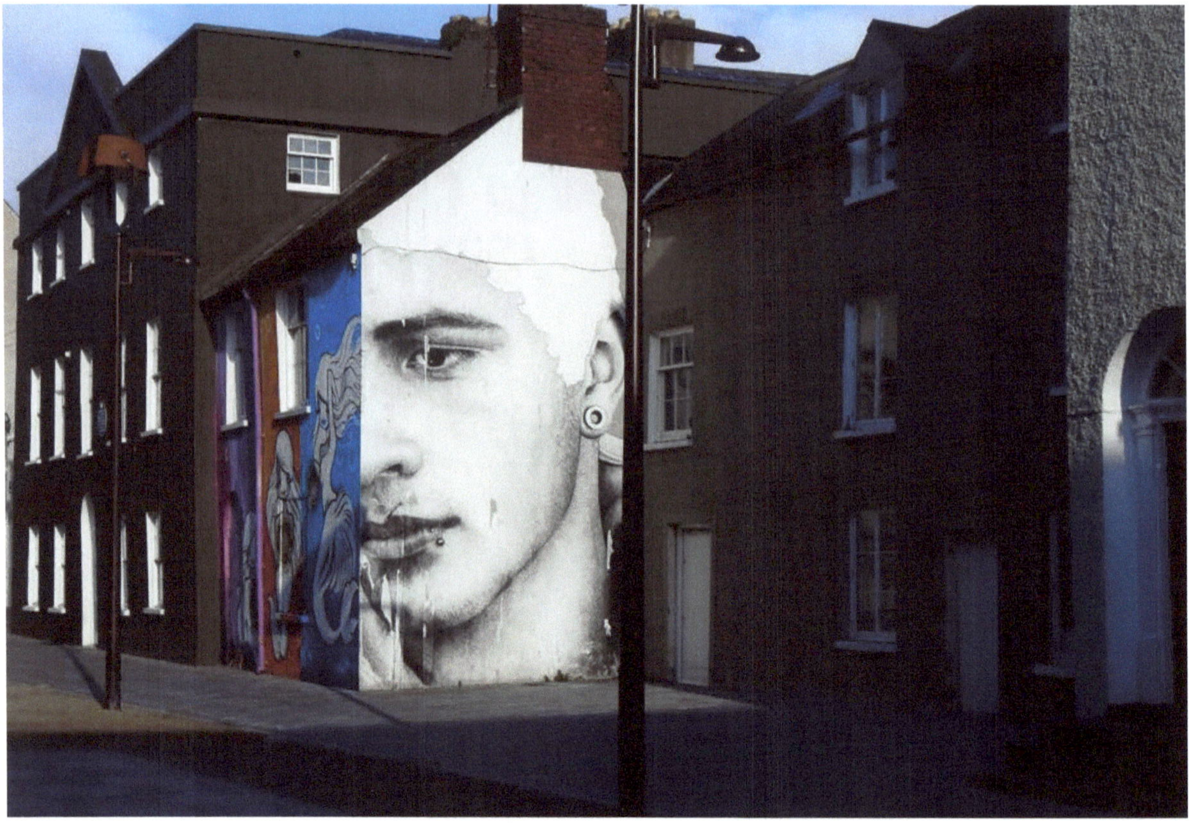

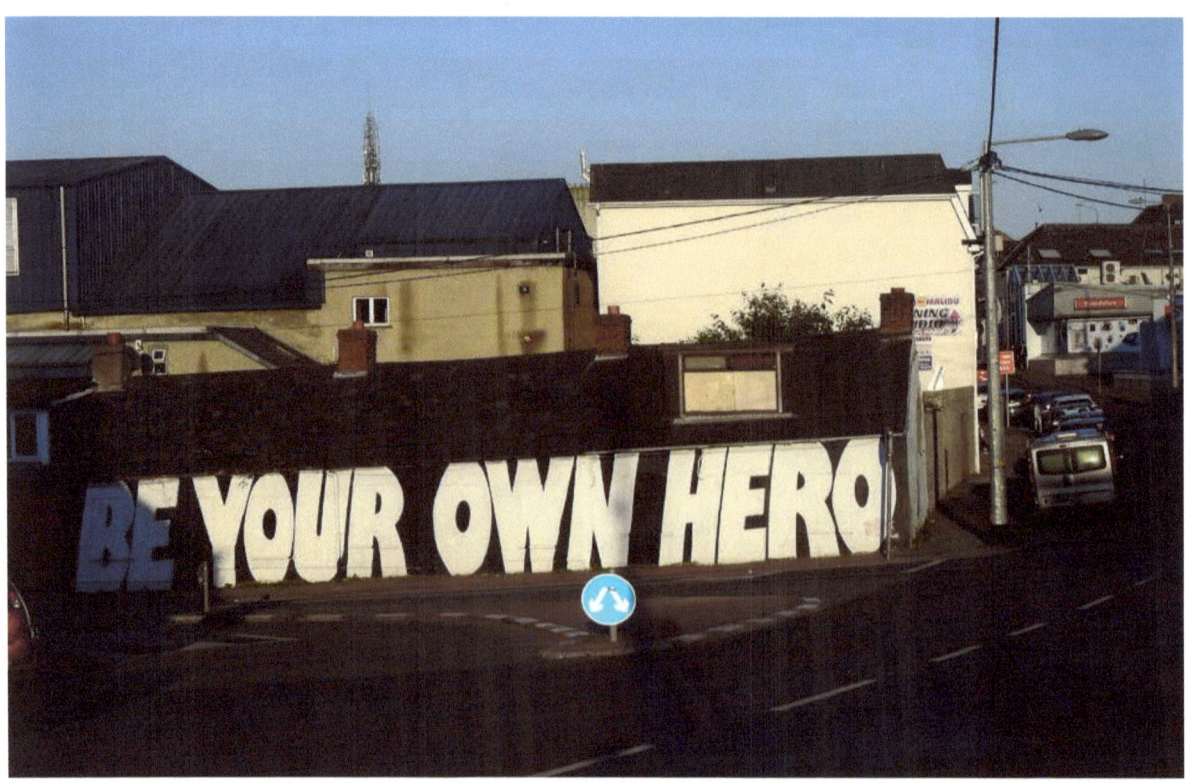

Waterford –The Untaken City

Opposite (Top): Wall Art located at Cathedral Square, Waterford City.

Opposite (Bottom): More art from the Waterford Walls project. Pictured near the Glen.

Opposite (Top): "End of Line". A cat sits on a quiet Platform No. 3 at Plunkett station Waterford. To commemorate the 1916 Rising, the station was named Plunkett station in honor of Joseph Plunkett.

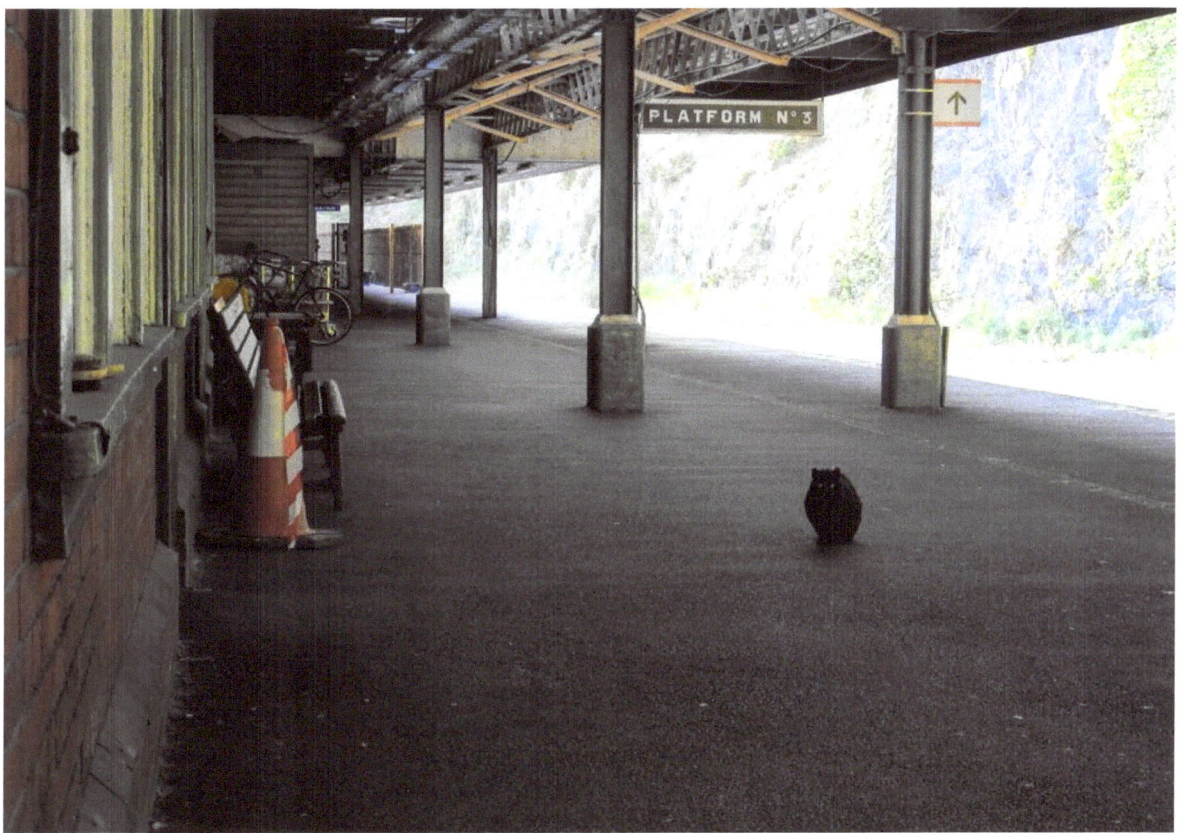

Opposite (Top): " The Bullpost" on Ballybricken. Locally known as the Hill.

Opposite (Bottom): An traditional shop front is maintained in excellent condition.

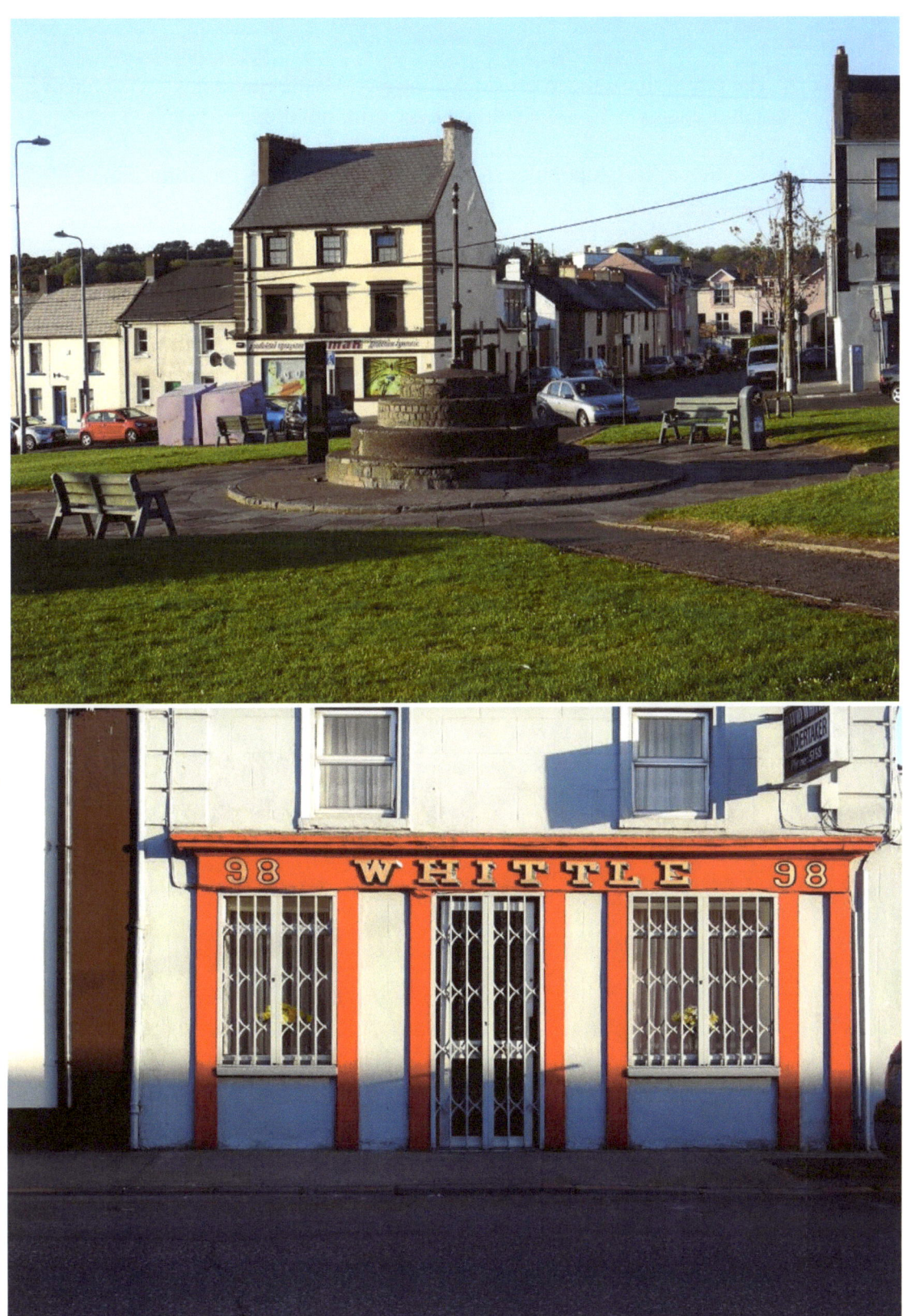

Opposite (Top): The city walls at the West side of the city. Castle Street has two defensive towers that are structurally in very good condition even after hundreds of years.

Opposite (Bottom): "Siopa Ris" A popular stop for the local students of Mount Sion CBS.

Below: The bandstand at Ballybricken.

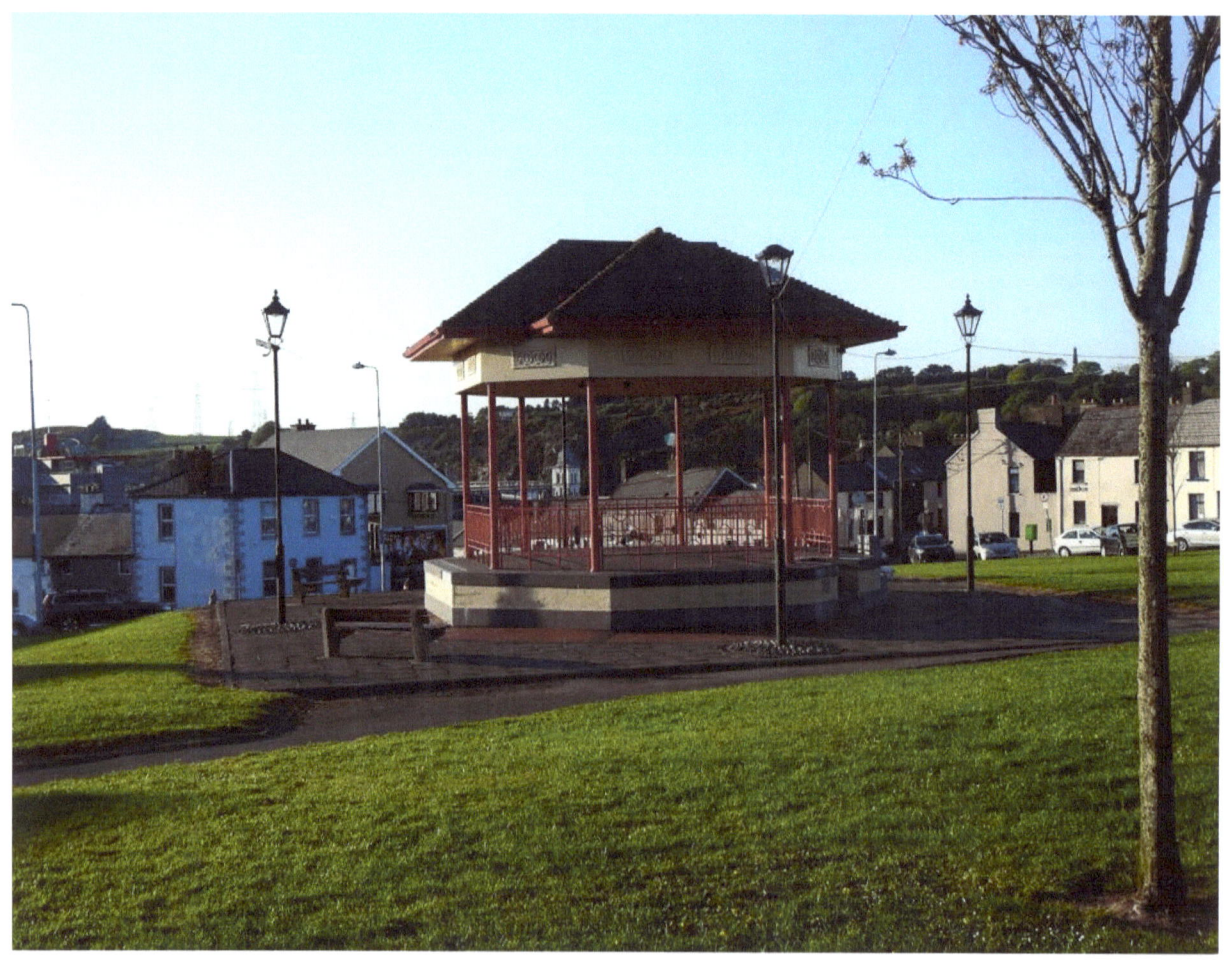

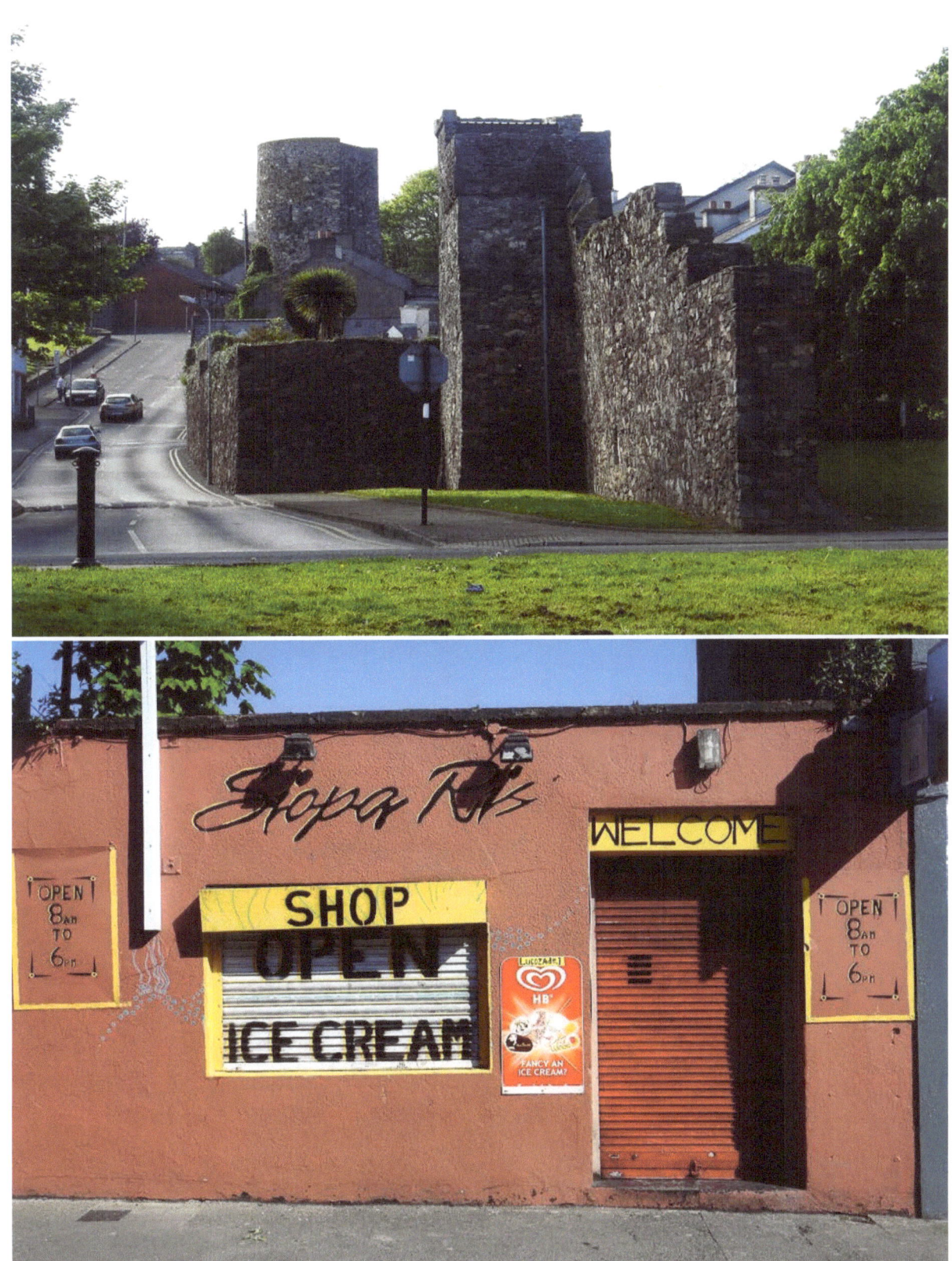

Waterford –The Untaken City

Opposite : A young bird with mixed plumage. Pictured on the Marina pontoon.

Below: The remains of the old mill buildings along the North Quays of Waterford City.

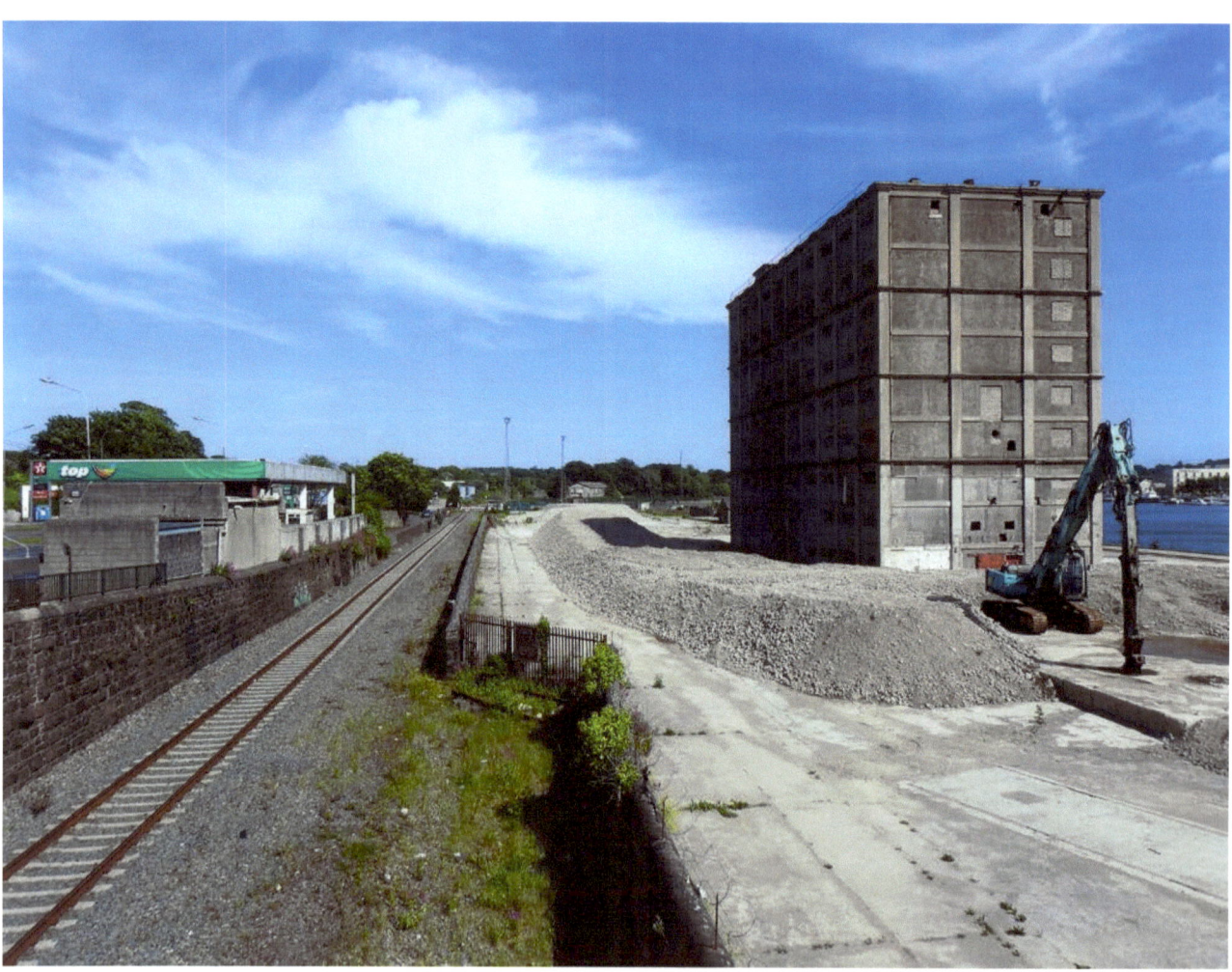

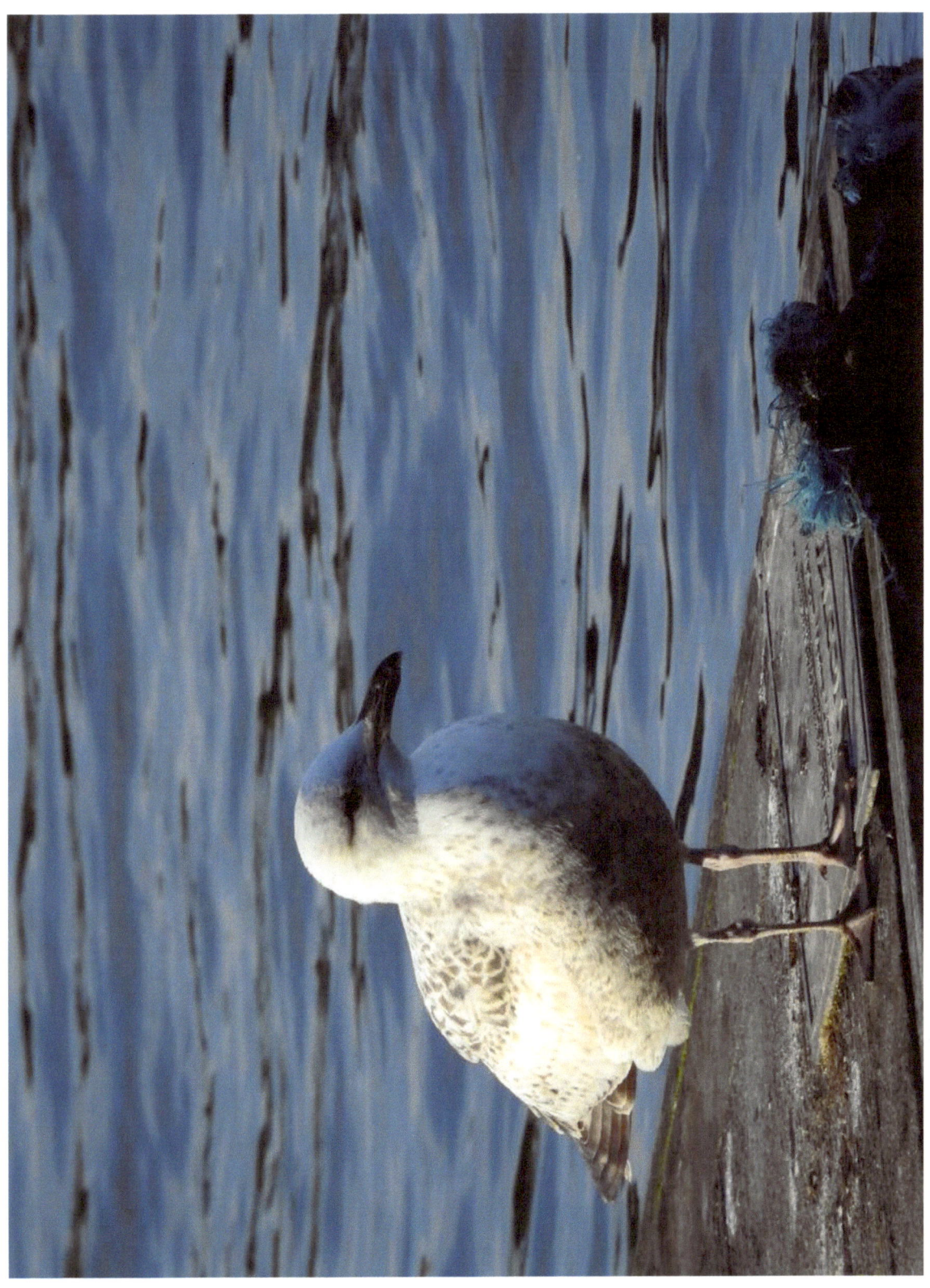

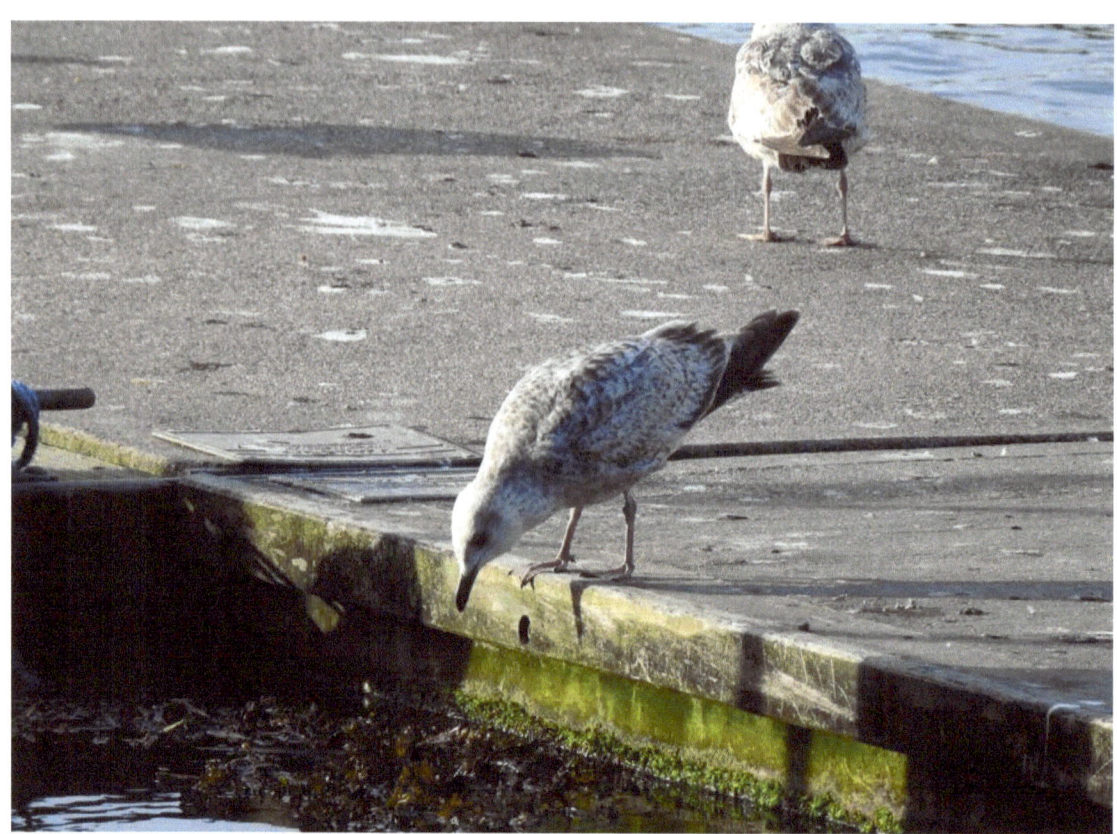

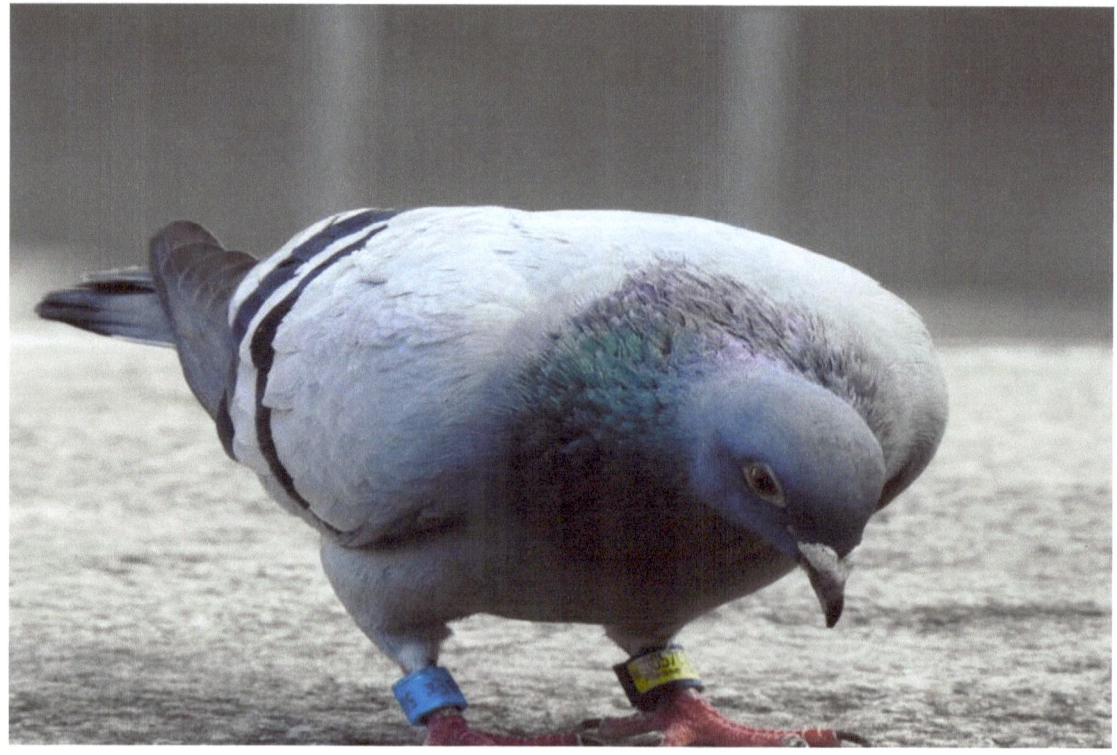

Opposite (Top): The Marina positions along the quayside make an ideal feeding position for birds.

Opposite (Bottom): A common pigeon

Below: A round tower on the city's eastside, close to Railway Square.

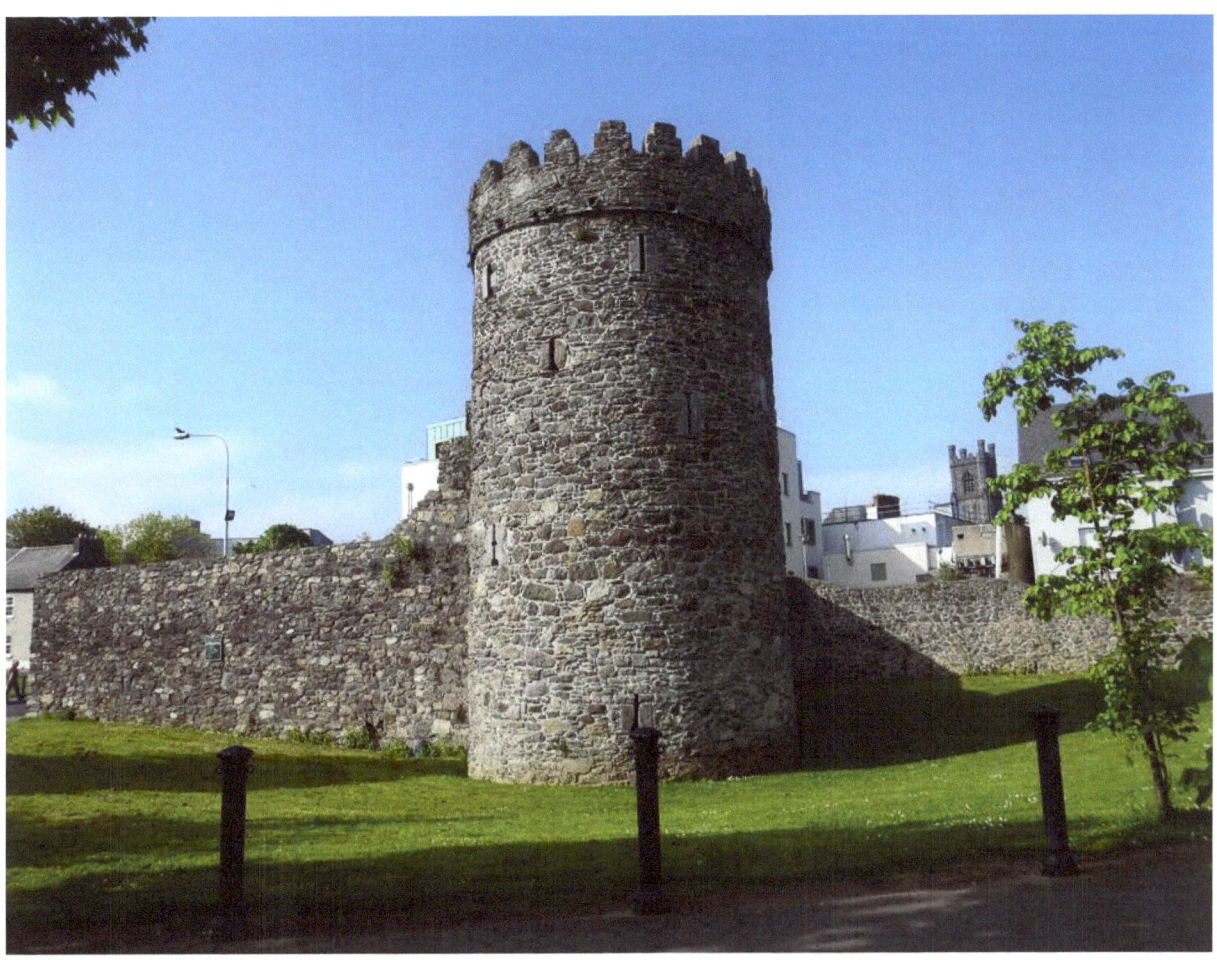

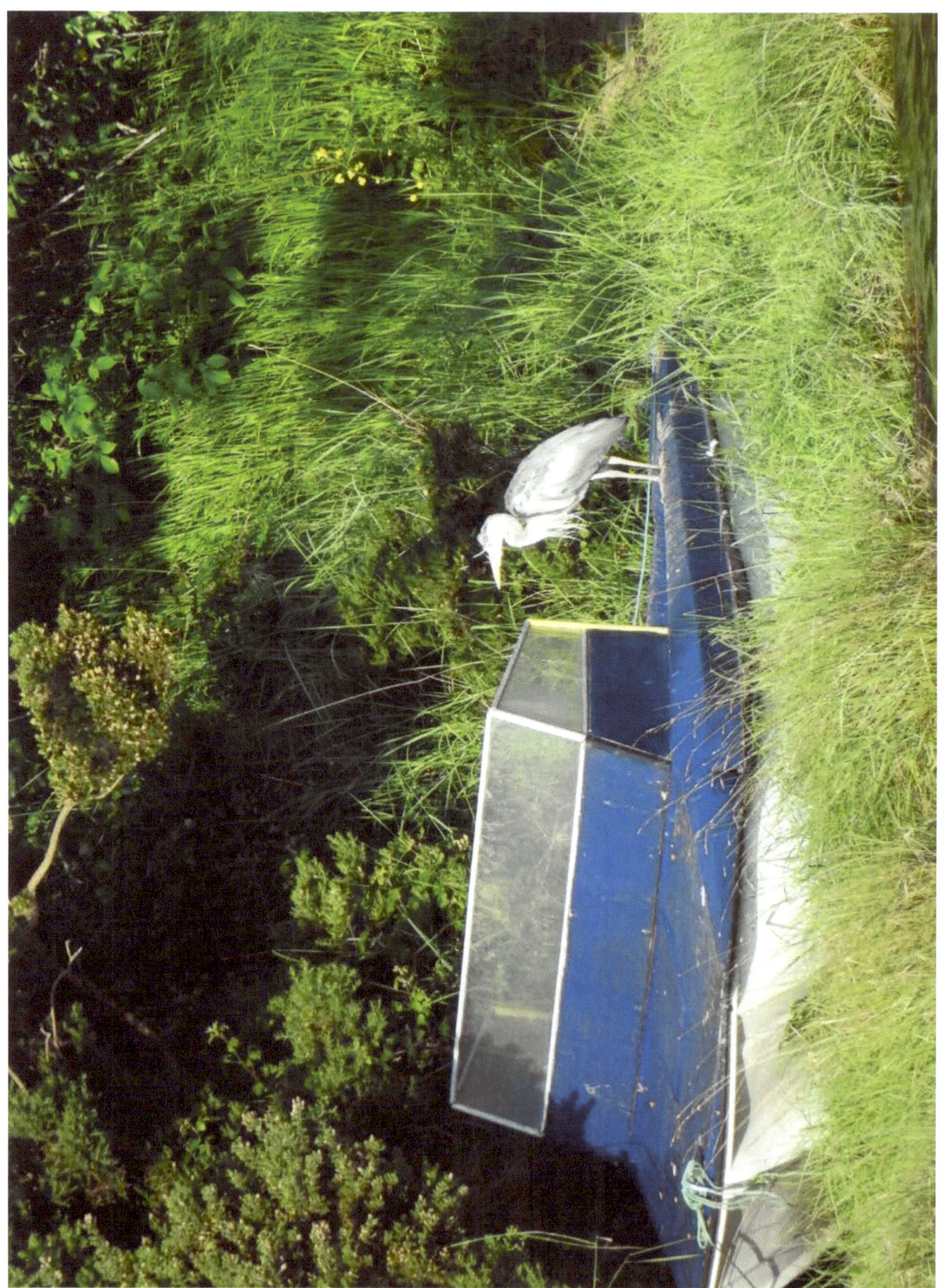

Opposite: A grey Heron perched on a small boat on the Ferrybank side of the river Suir. The area is known as Estuary wood. The Grey Heron remained in the same location for almost an hour, only moving its neck to inspect its plumage. Typically Grey Herons are seen in pairs, on this particular day two pairs were within 20-30 meters of one another.

Below: The Presentation Sisters Convent, pictured from Keane's Road

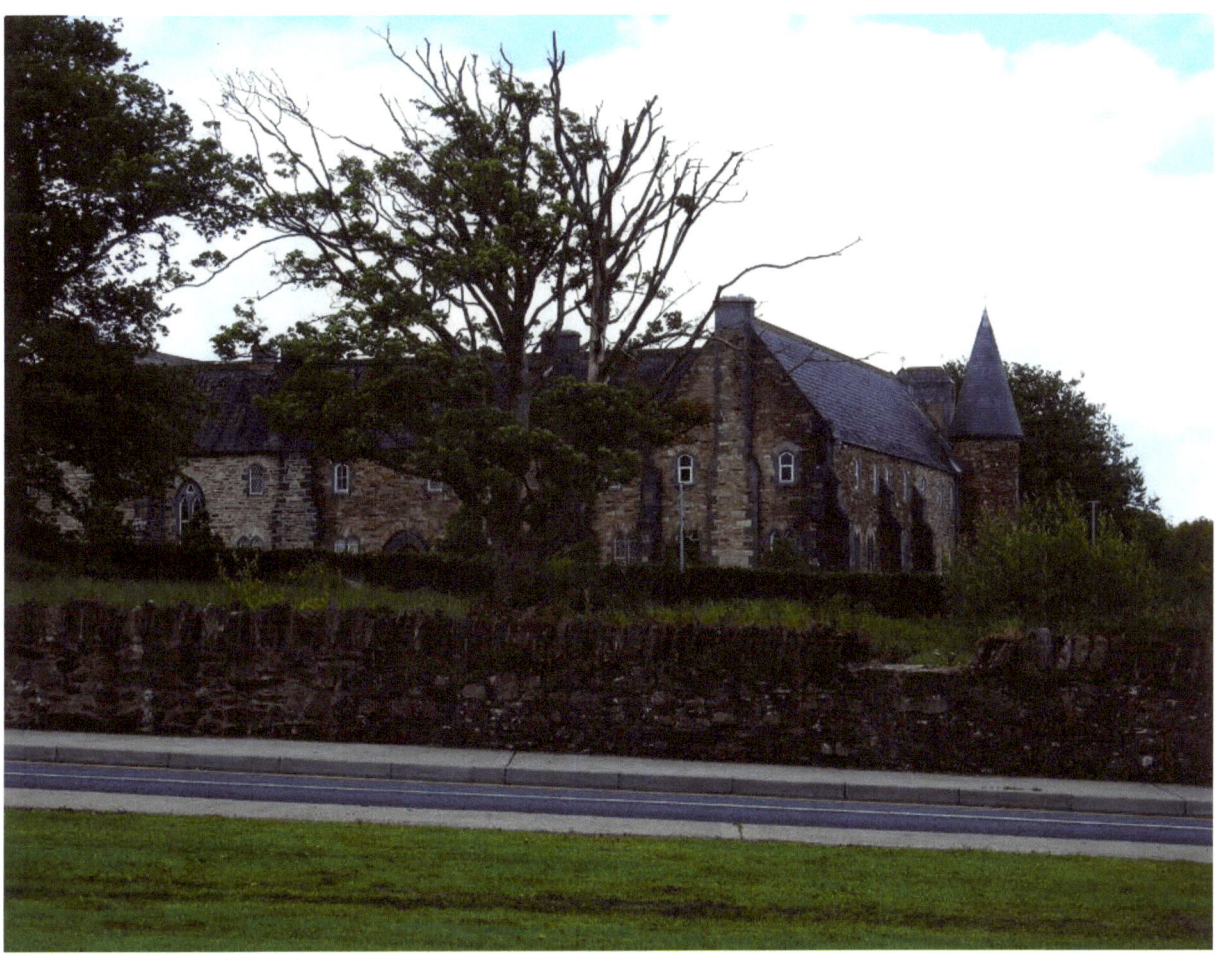

Waterford –The Untaken City

Opposite: A small jetty on the north side of the river Suir. Estuary Wood has limited access from the main road. It provides a quiet and peaceful environment for birds and wildlife.

Below: A mural at Plunkett Station details the first verse of the everlasting poem by Joseph Mary Plunkett, "I see his blood upon the Rose"

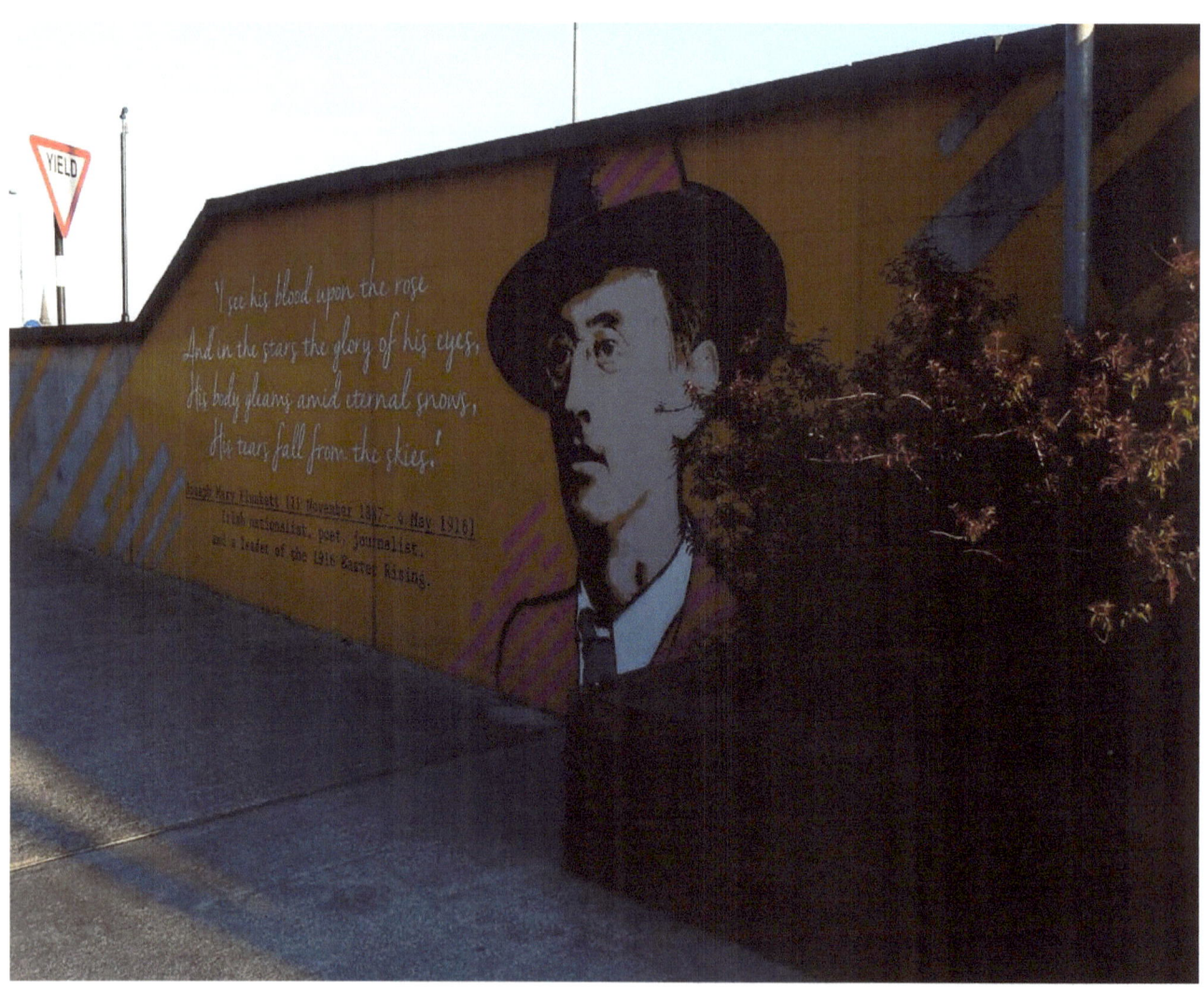

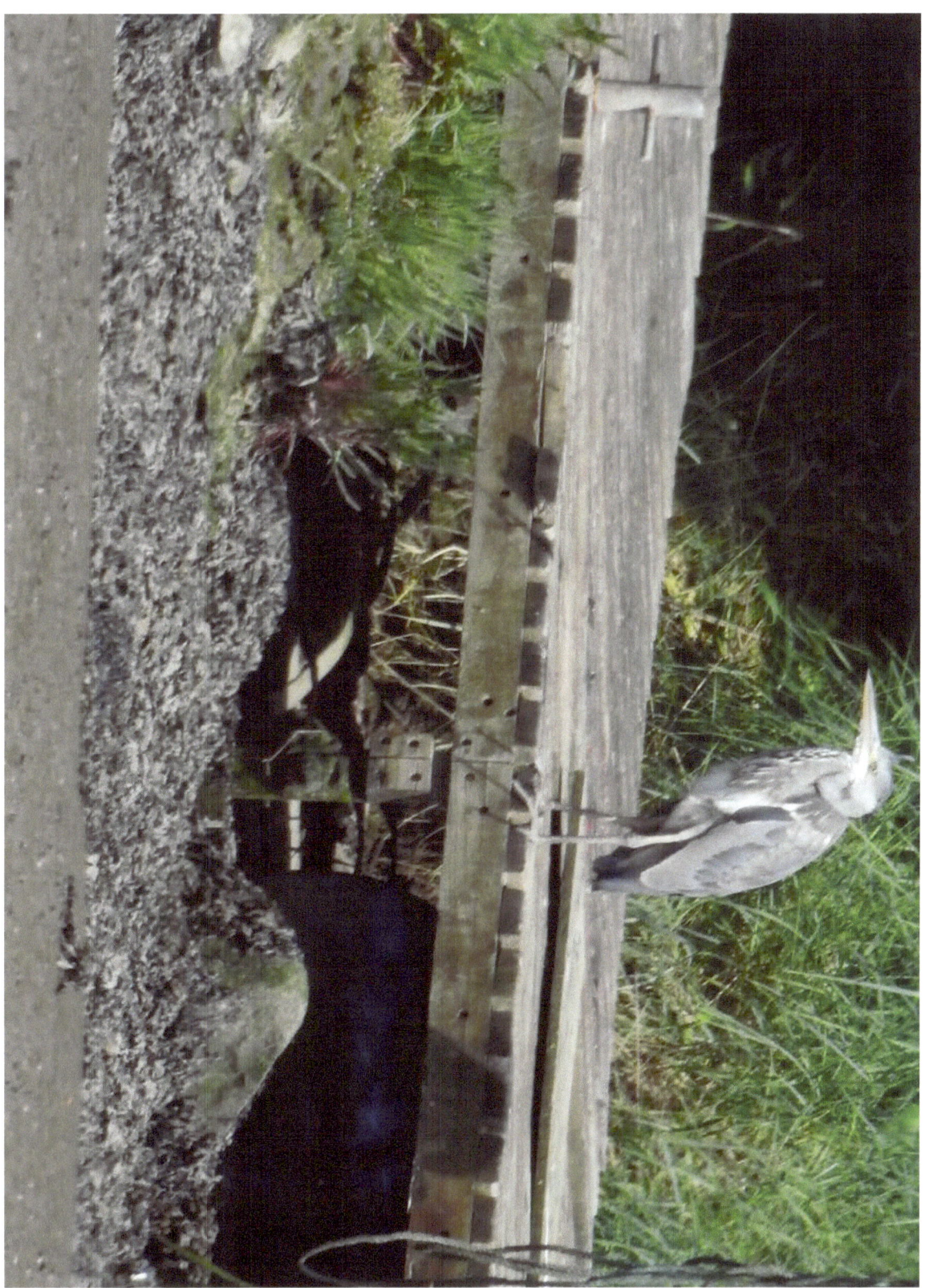

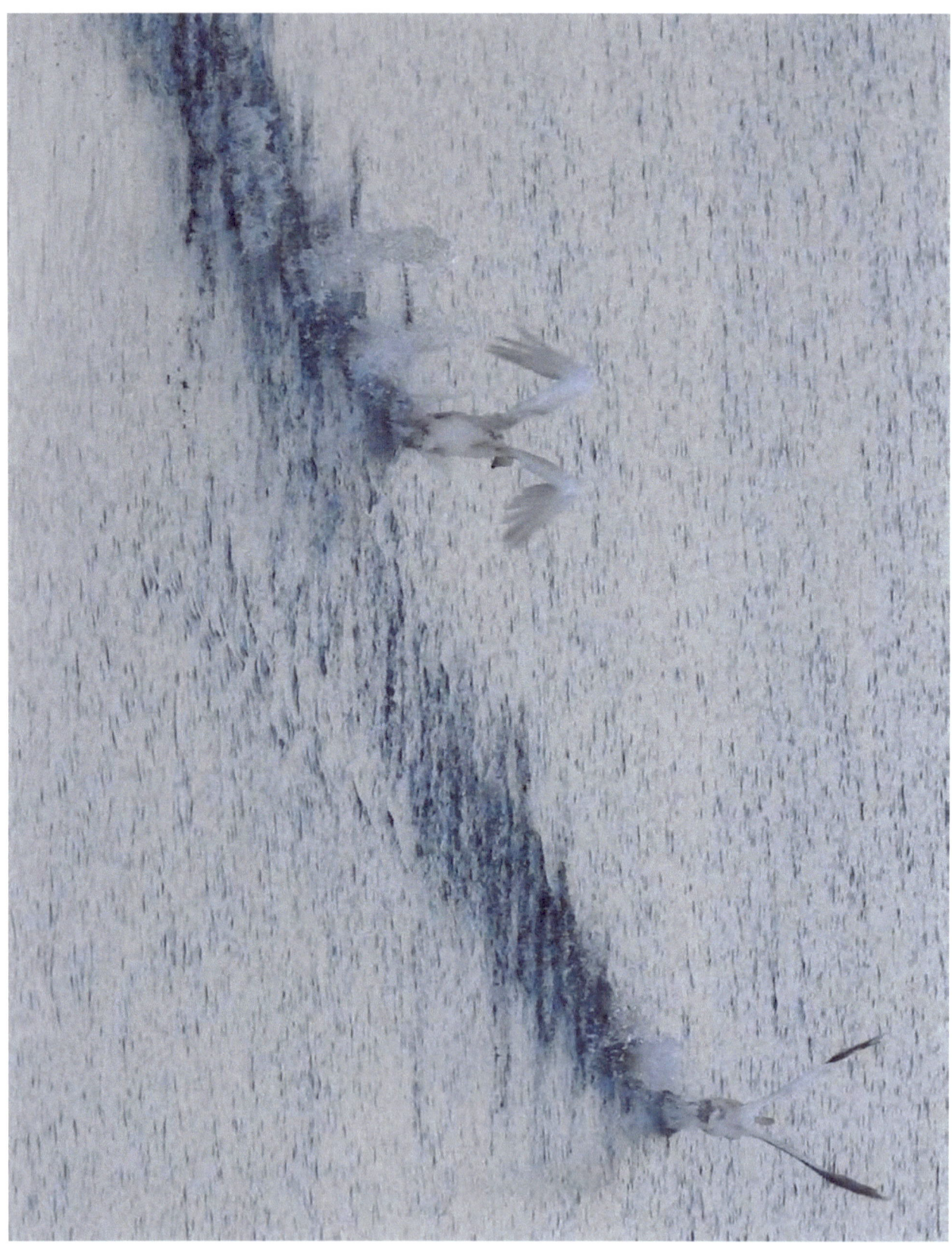

Opposite (Top): Swans break into flight on the River Suir at evening time.

Below: Baileys New Street.

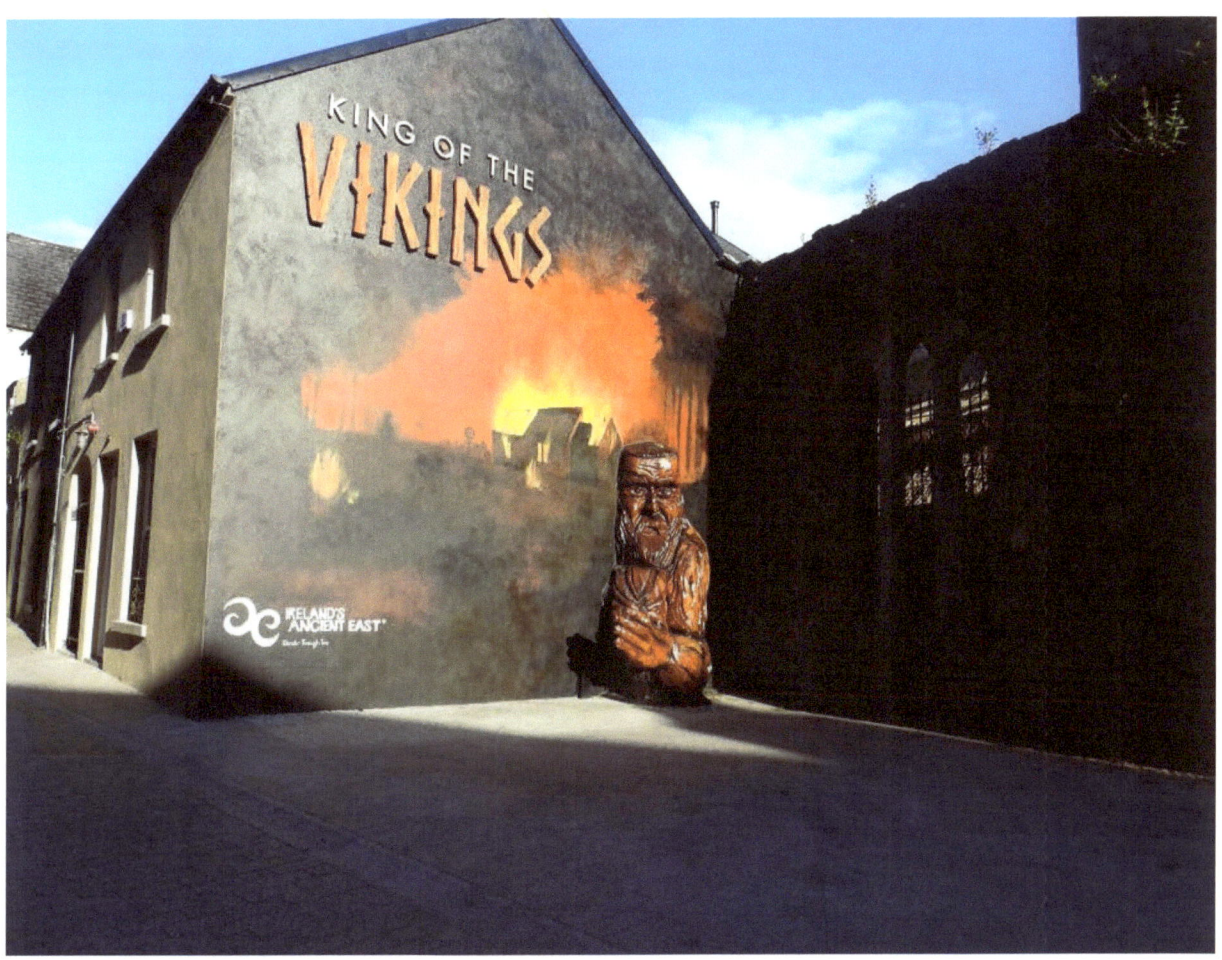

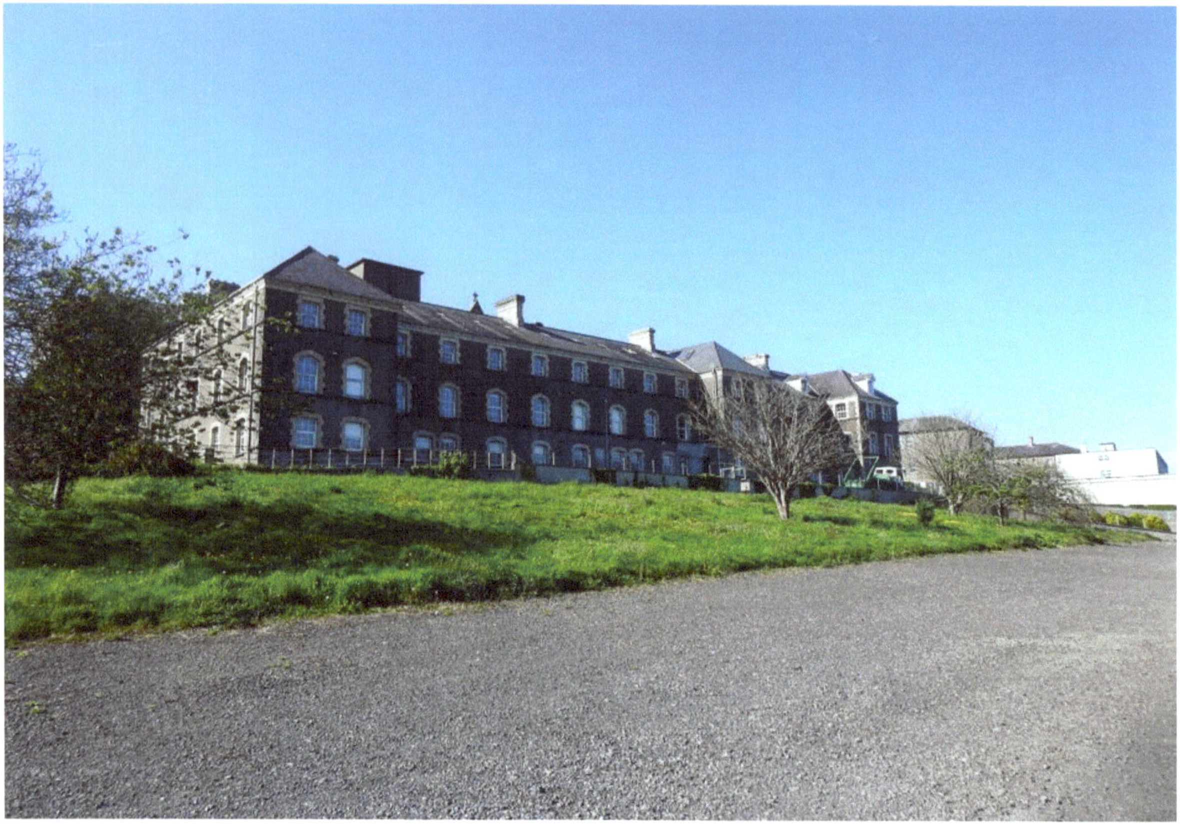

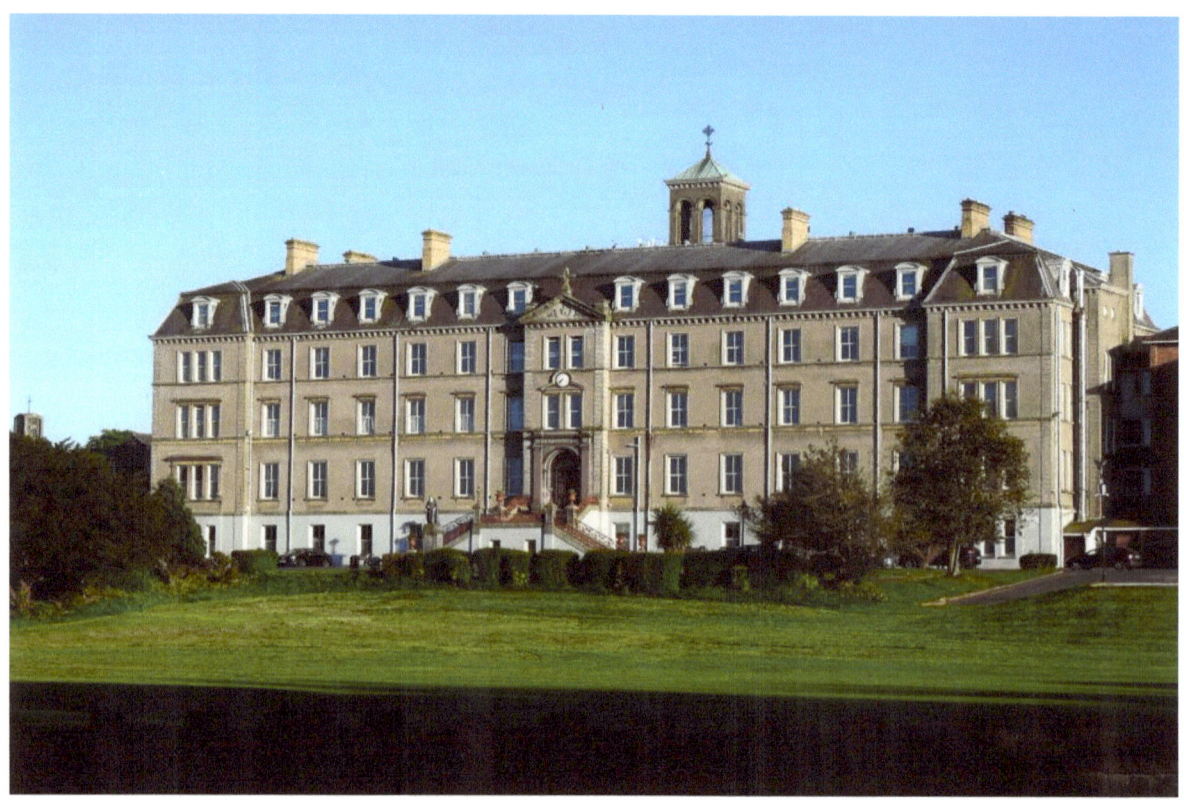

Waterford – The Untaken City

Opposite (Top): The now vacant Little Sisters of the Poor, Saint Joseph's House.

Opposite (Bottom): De la Salle college, situated opposite the People's Park.

Below: The scenic and peaceful view from Canada Square in the direction of the coast.

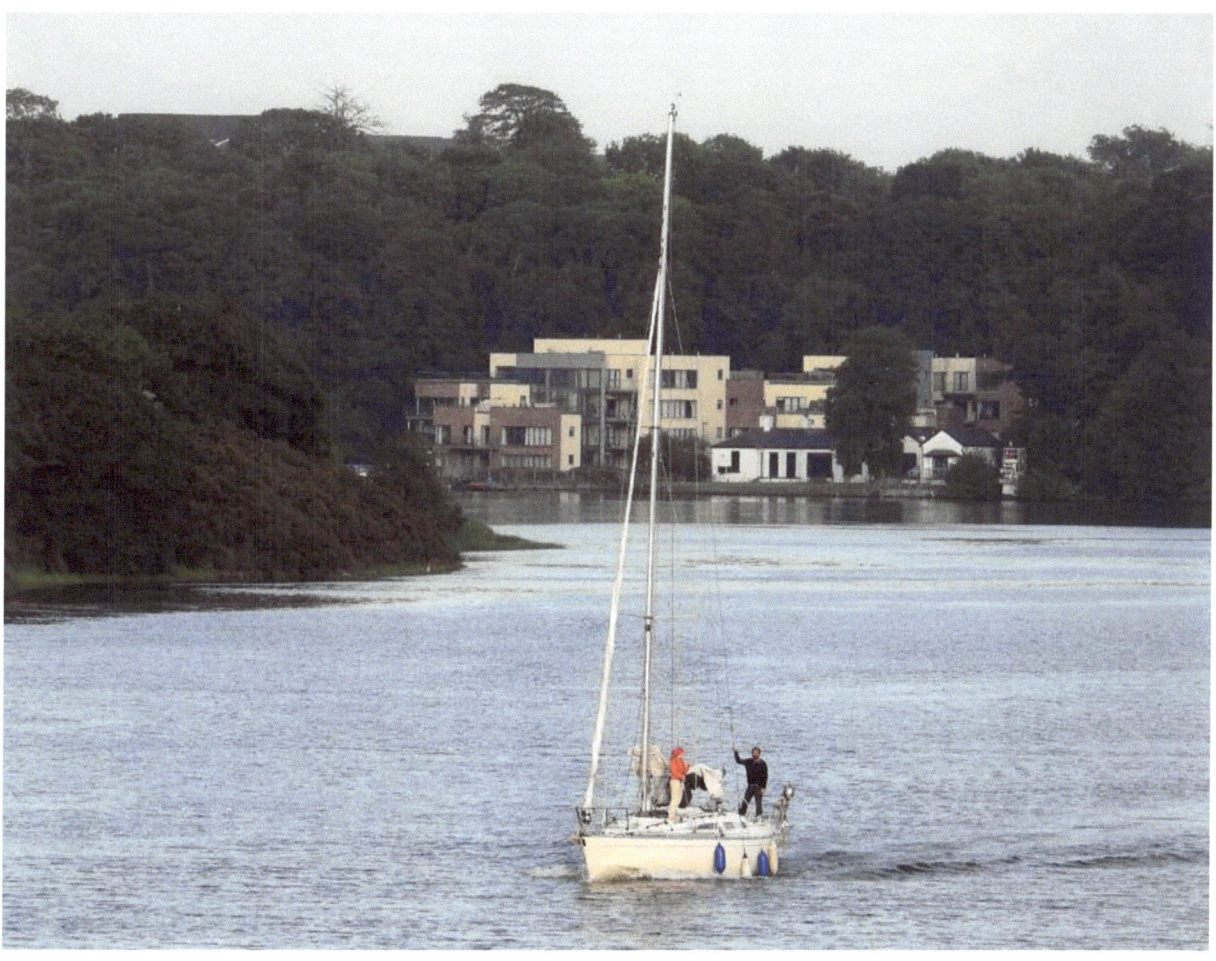

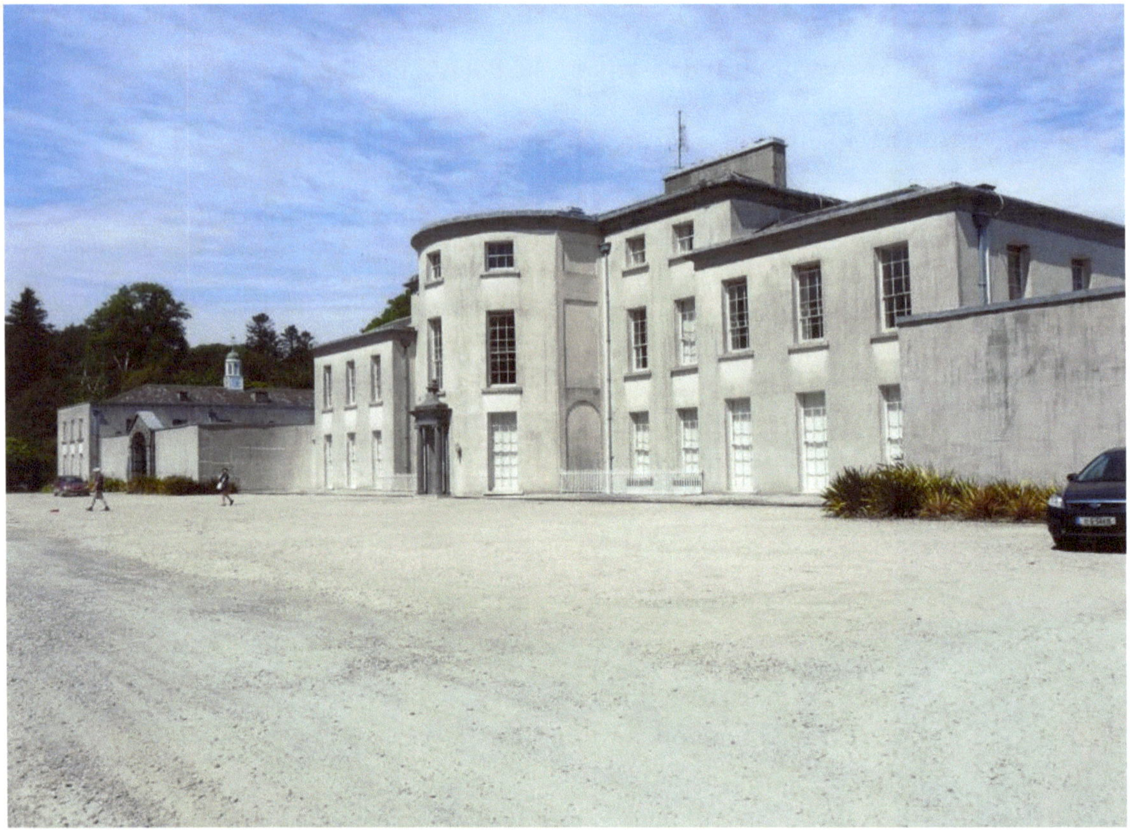

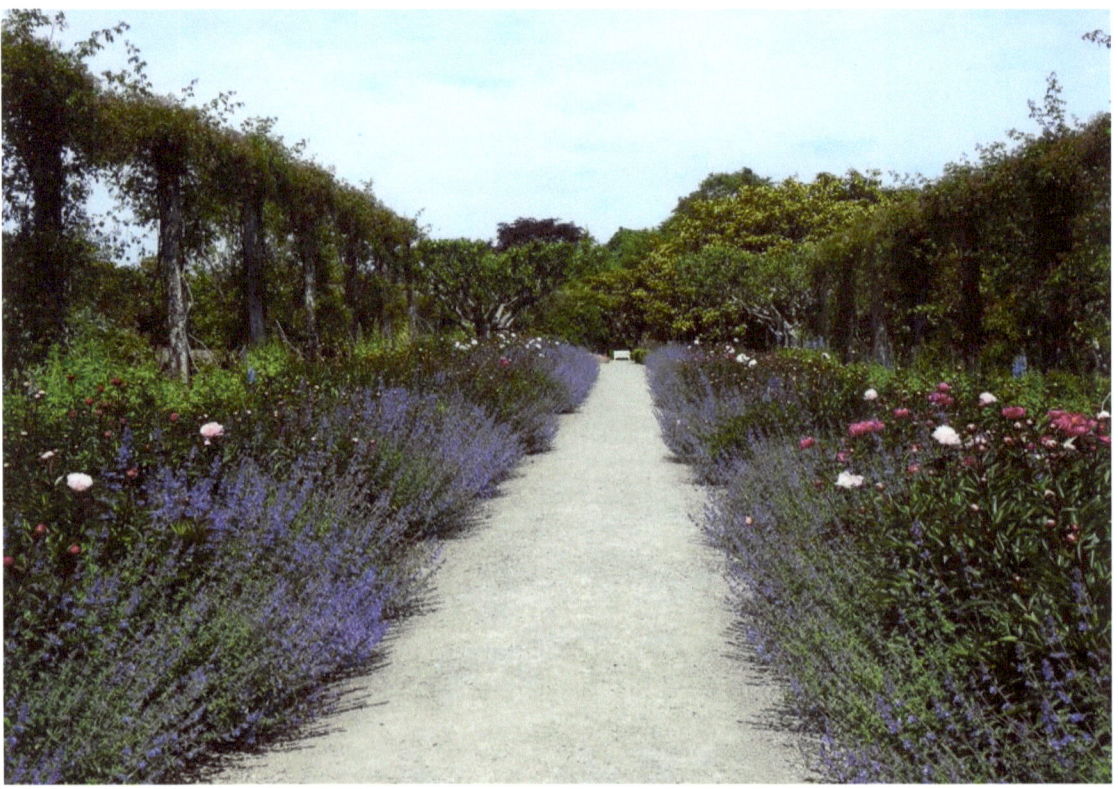

Waterford –The Untaken City

Opposite (Top): Mount Congreve Estate, Kilmeaden, Co. Waterford.

Opposite (Bottom): Mount Congreve estate has over 70 acres of woodland gardens and a 4 acre walled garden.

Below: Walsh Park, GAA Grounds. named after Willie Walsh, a well-known referee and long time campaigner for Gaelic games in Waterford.

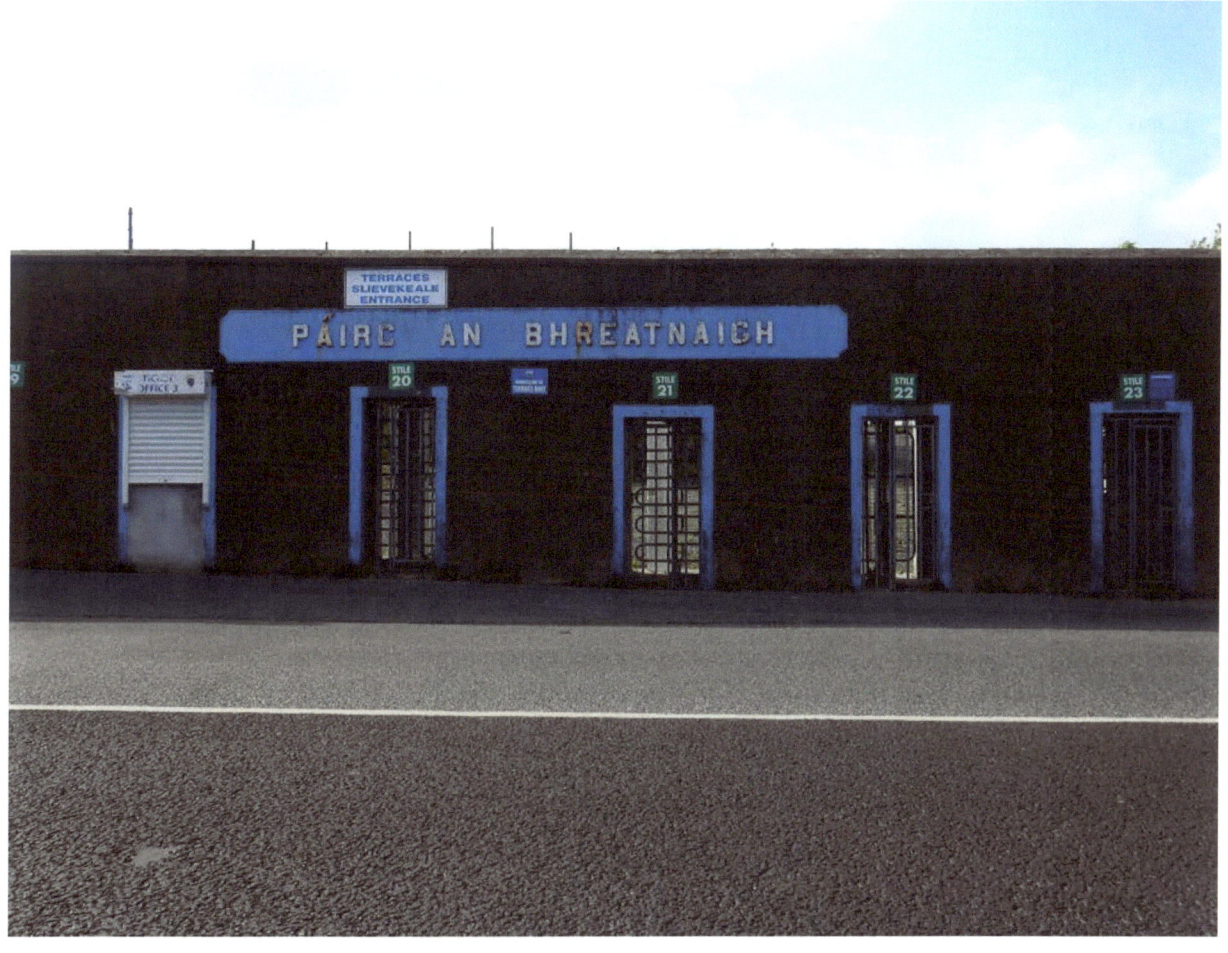

Waterford –The Untaken City

Opposite (Top): J&K Walsh, 11 Georges Street.

Opposite (Bottom): Tom Mahers Pub, 20, O' Connell Street, Waterford City.

Below: Waterford Castle, situated on The Island. Home to a diverse mix of wildlife.

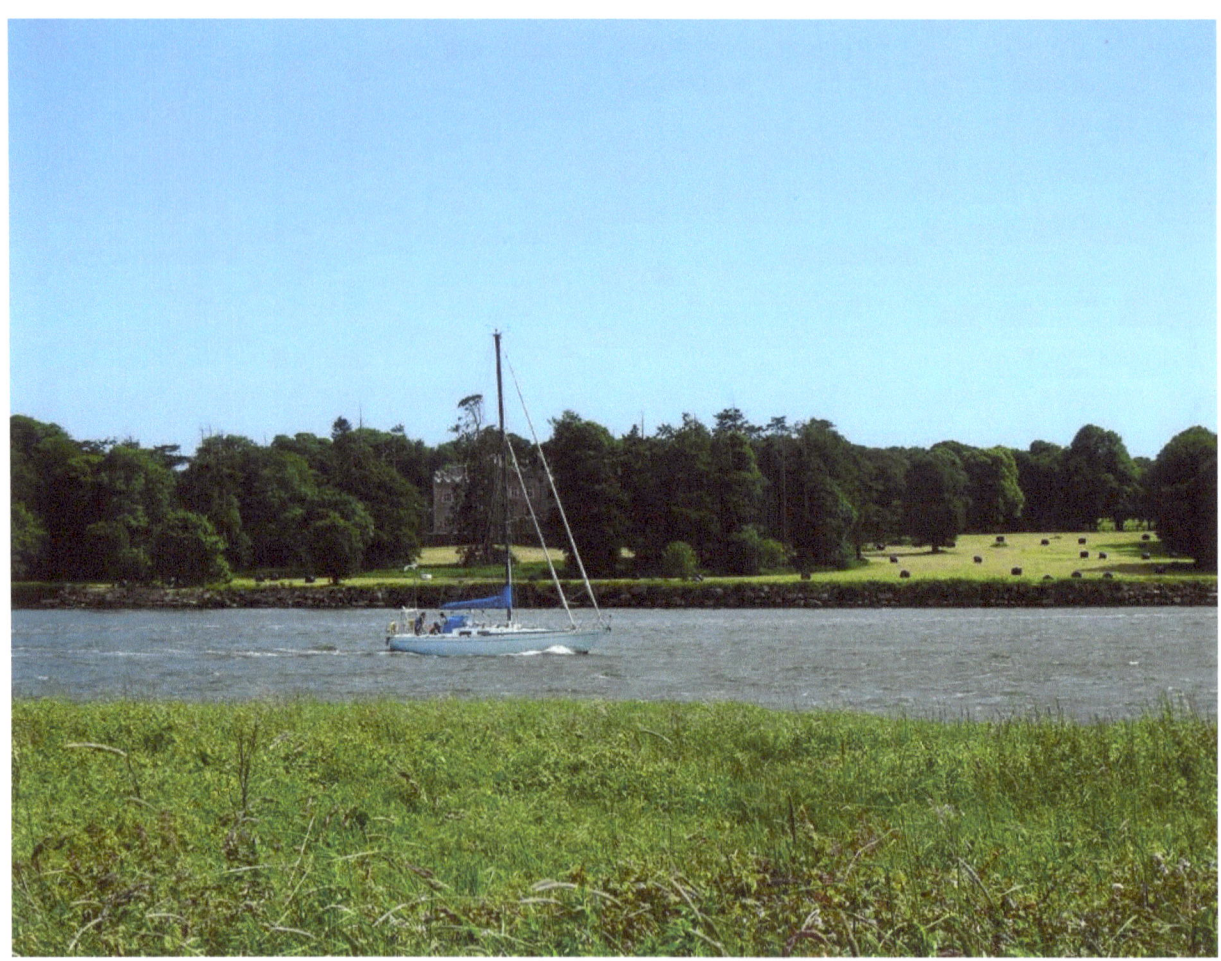

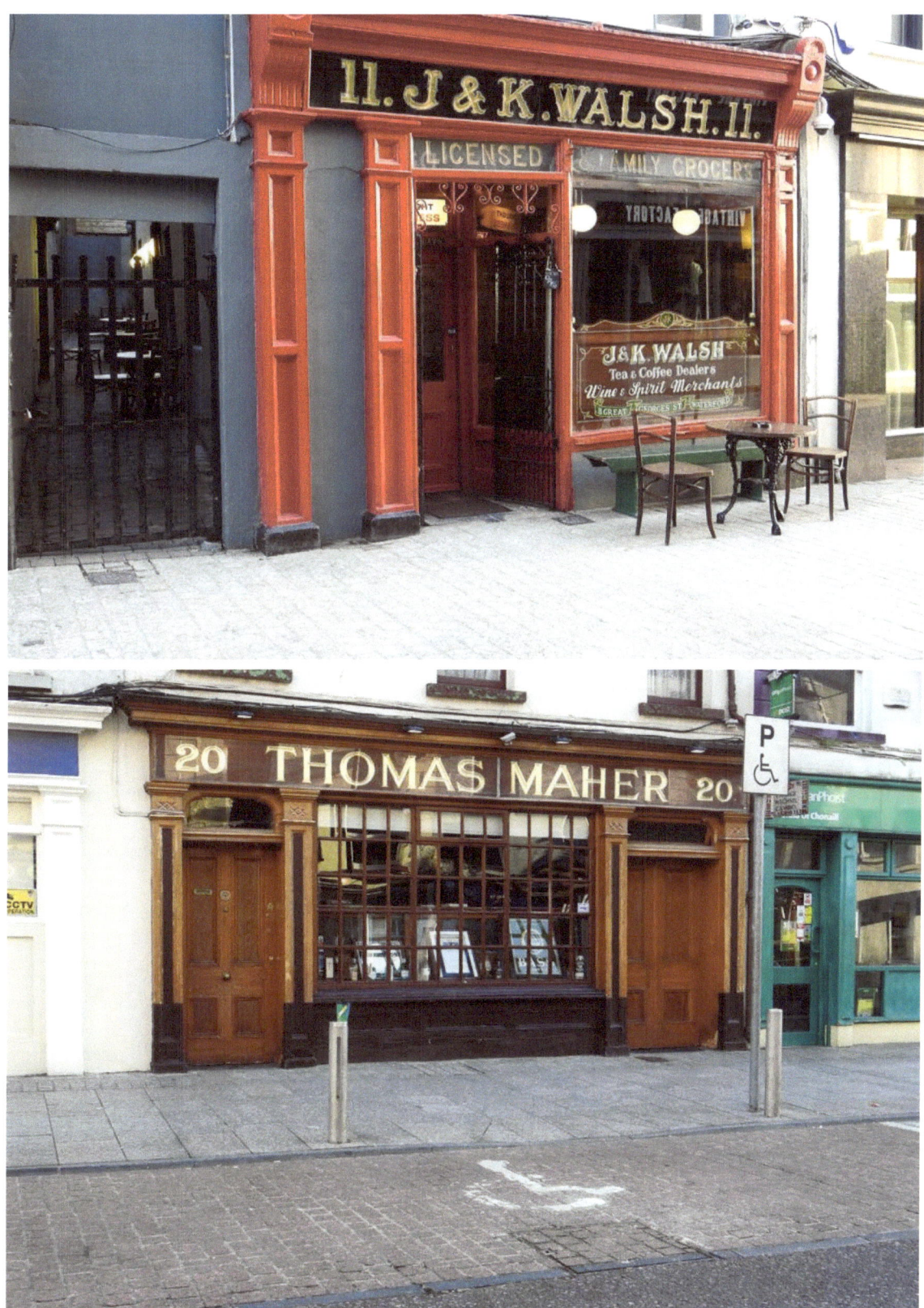

Opposite: John Roberts Square with the Clock Tower situated at the end of the street.

Below: The Tower Hotel pictured from Ferrybank.

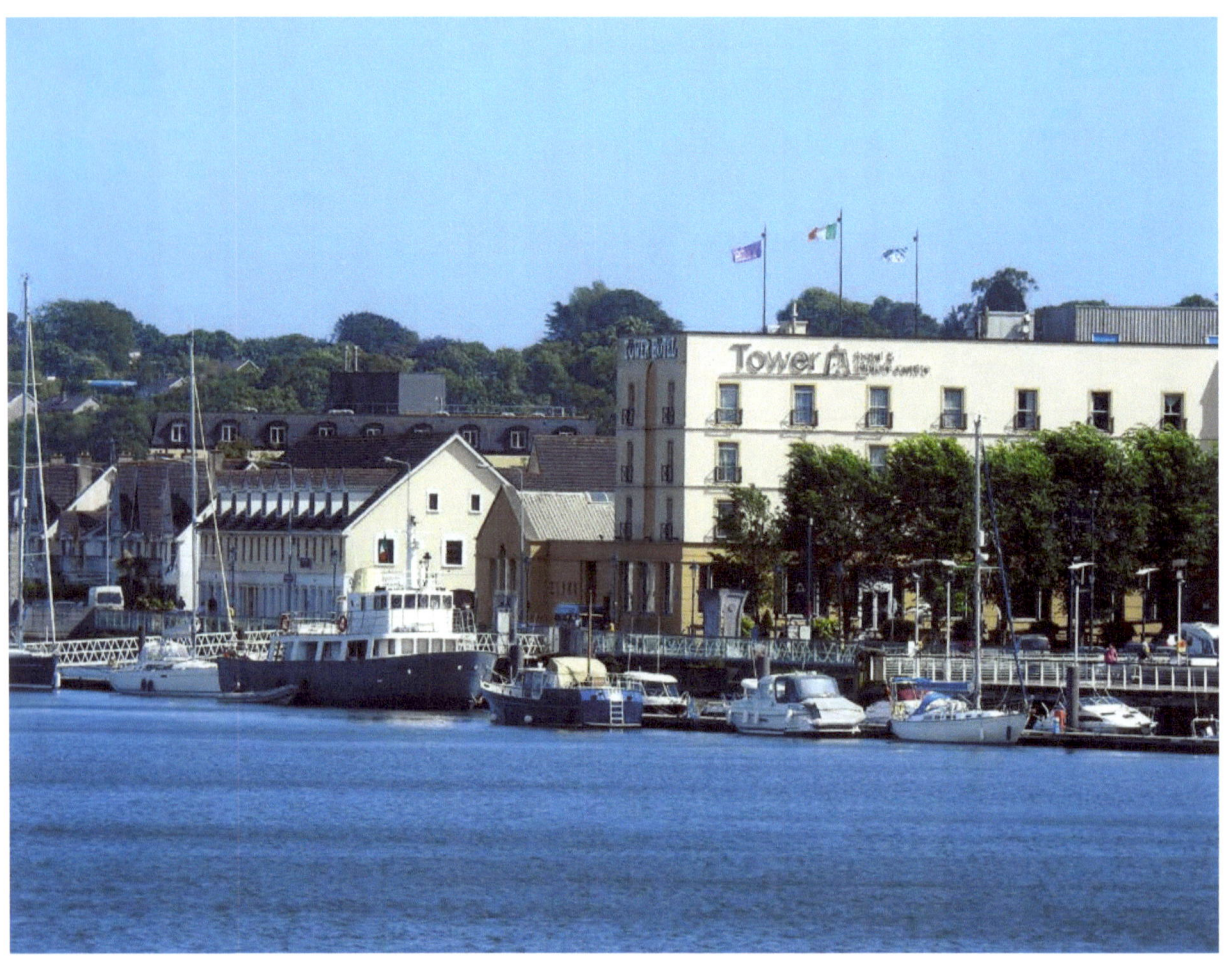

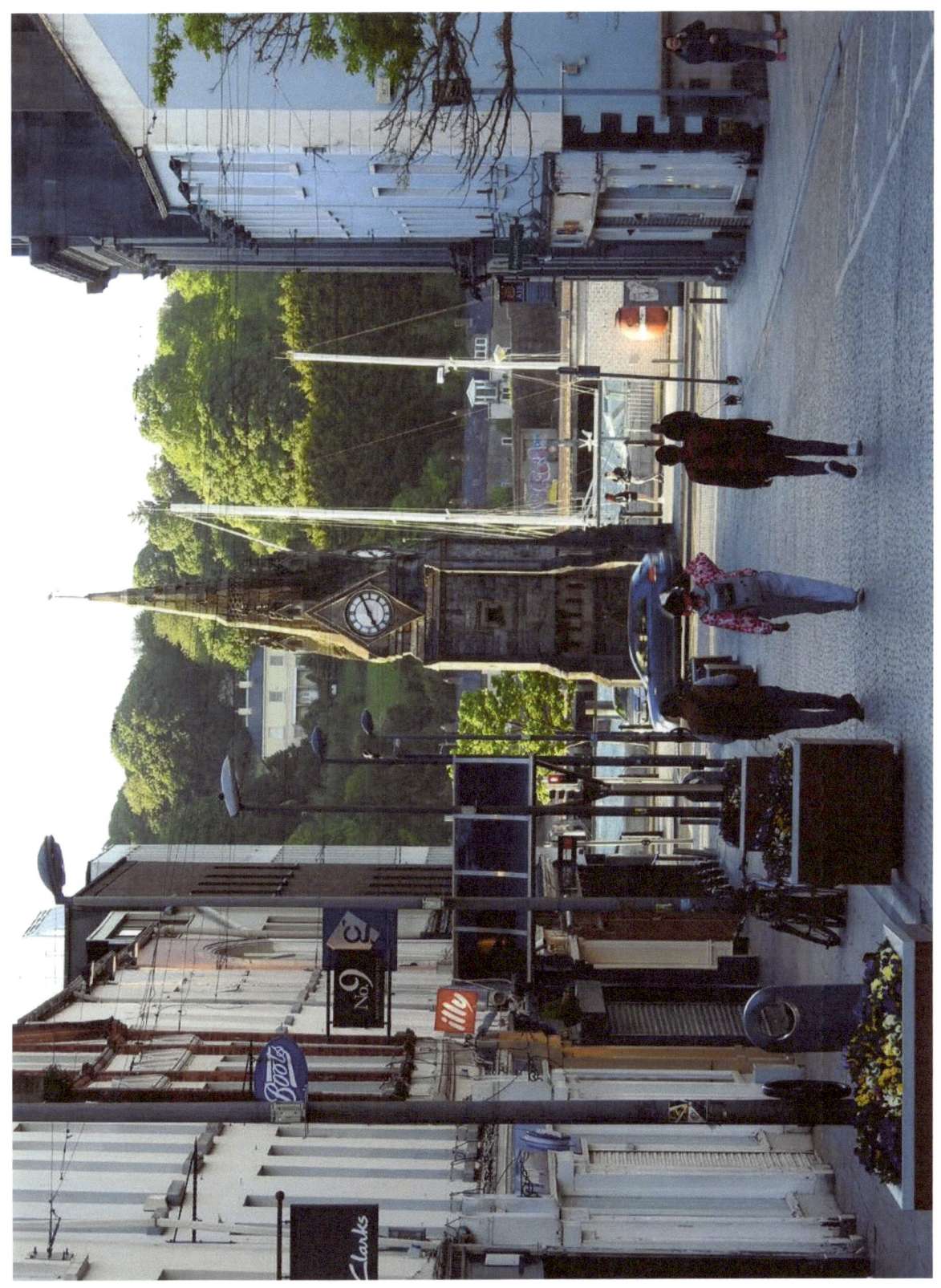

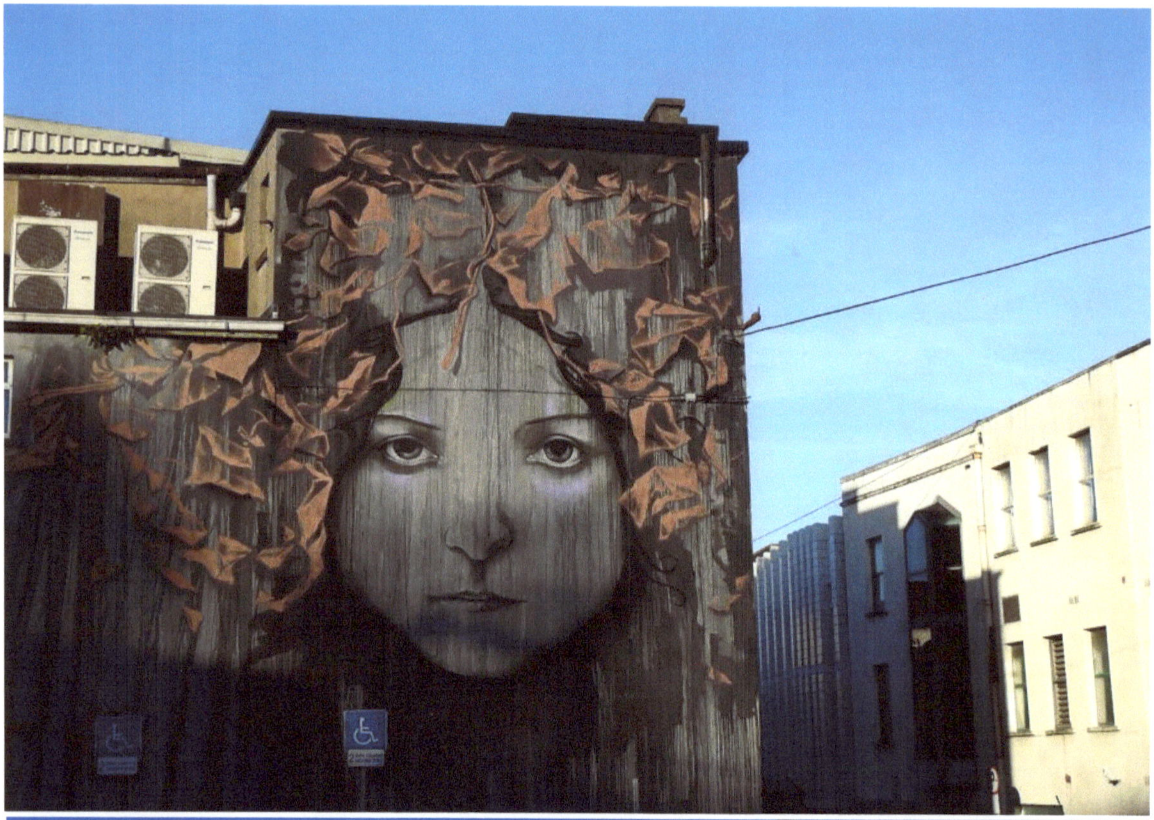

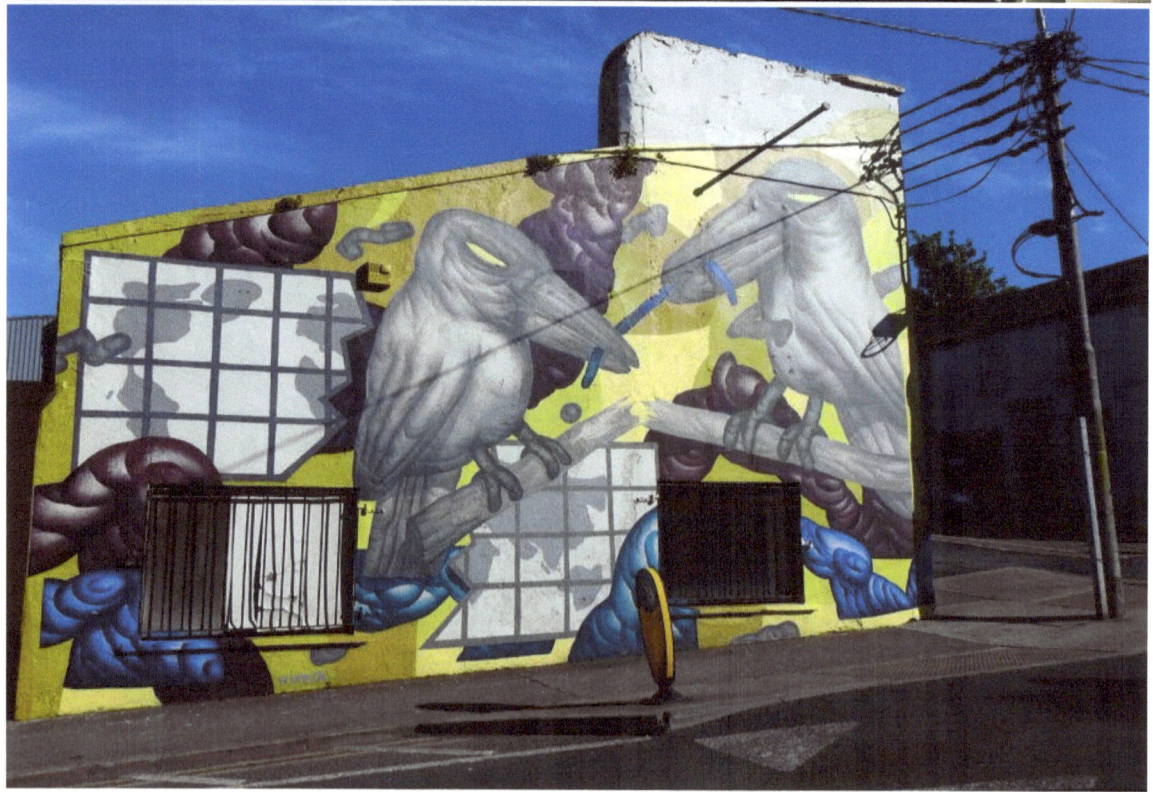

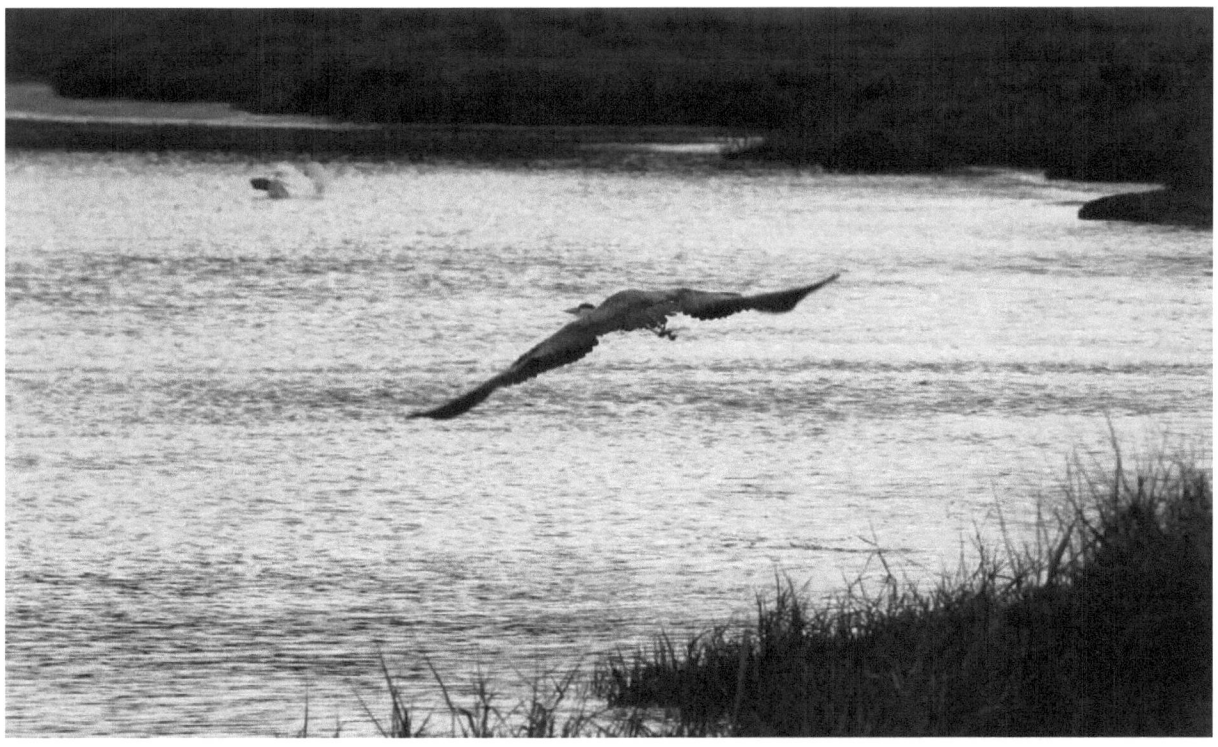

Above: A Grey Heron pictured at Kings Channel, Waterford City, flies slowly with heavy wing beats and legs outstretched behind. Cold winters often impact the populations.

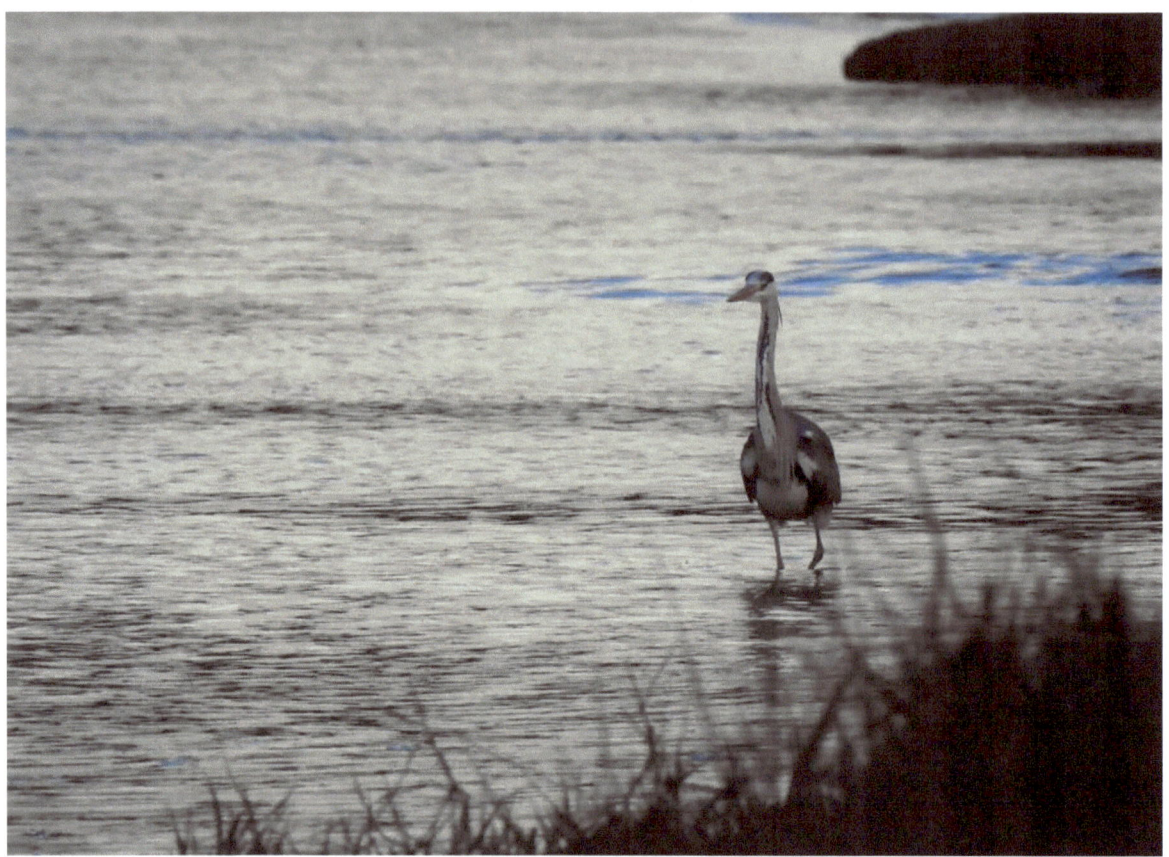

Above: With a mainly grey plumage and a black stripe above the eye, the Grey Heron feeds in shallow waters.

Waterford –The Untaken City

Below: Reginalds tower pictured from Ferrybank with the Marina at low tide.

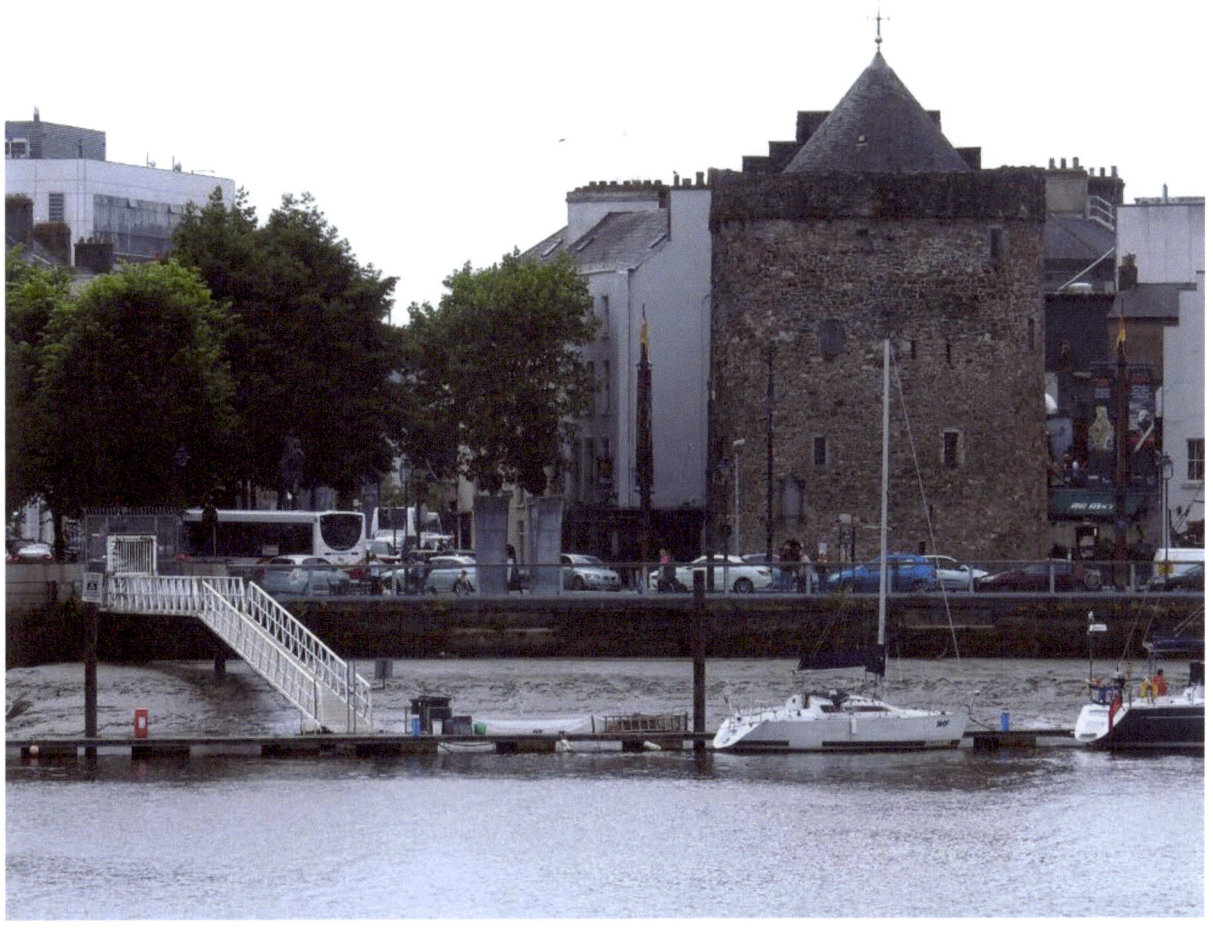

Waterford –The Untaken City

Opposite: Pictured from Cassin Wharf, a view of the Quayside in the city. To the far left, the tower of the old Franciscan monastery can be seen. Centre shot the steeple of Christ Church Cathedral. Slightly left of the Cathedrals steeple the tower of the current Franciscan Friary in Lady Lane.

Below: The Silver Explorer expedition ship departs from Cassin Wharf and heads down river towards Dunmore East. With a crew of 115 and a passenger capacity of 132, her small size makes it easier for her to navigate up river to the heart of the city.

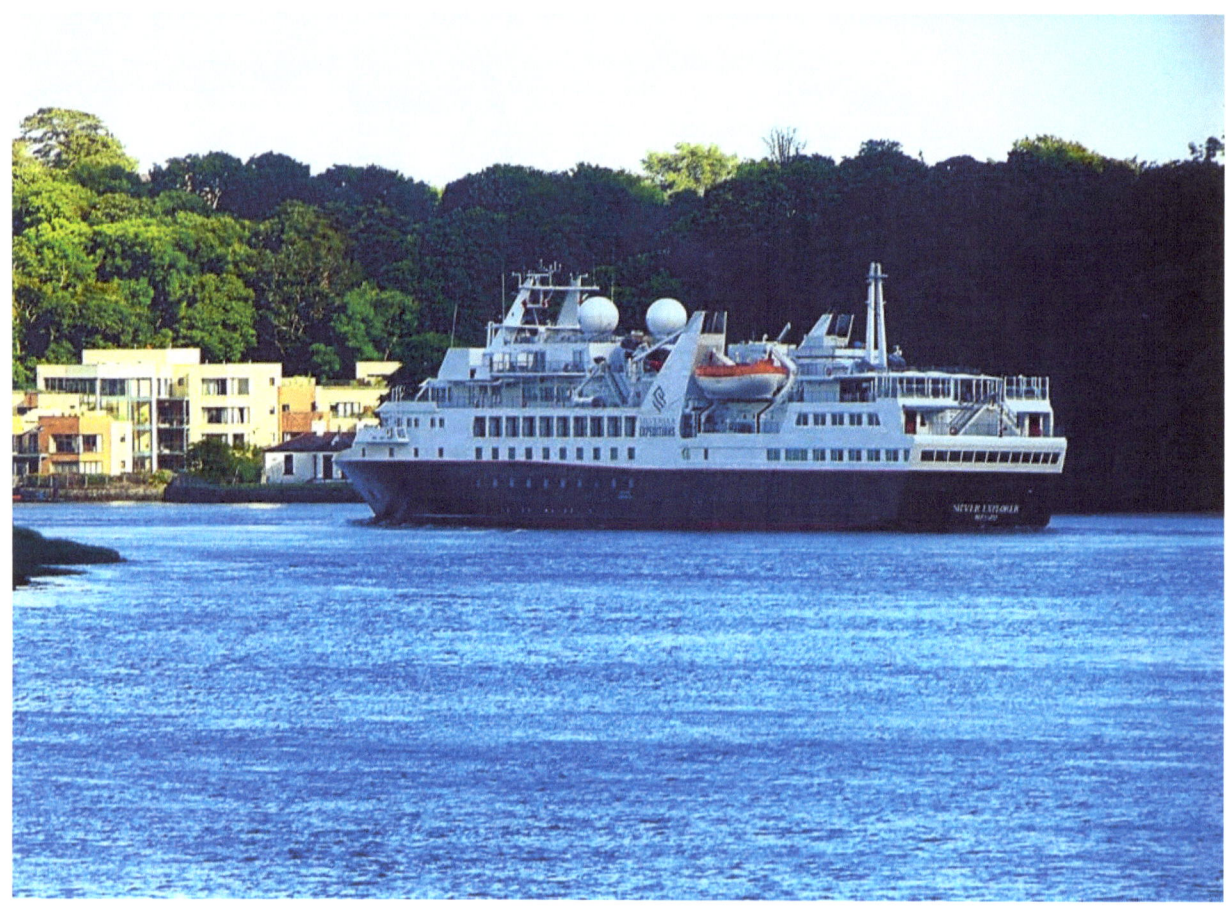

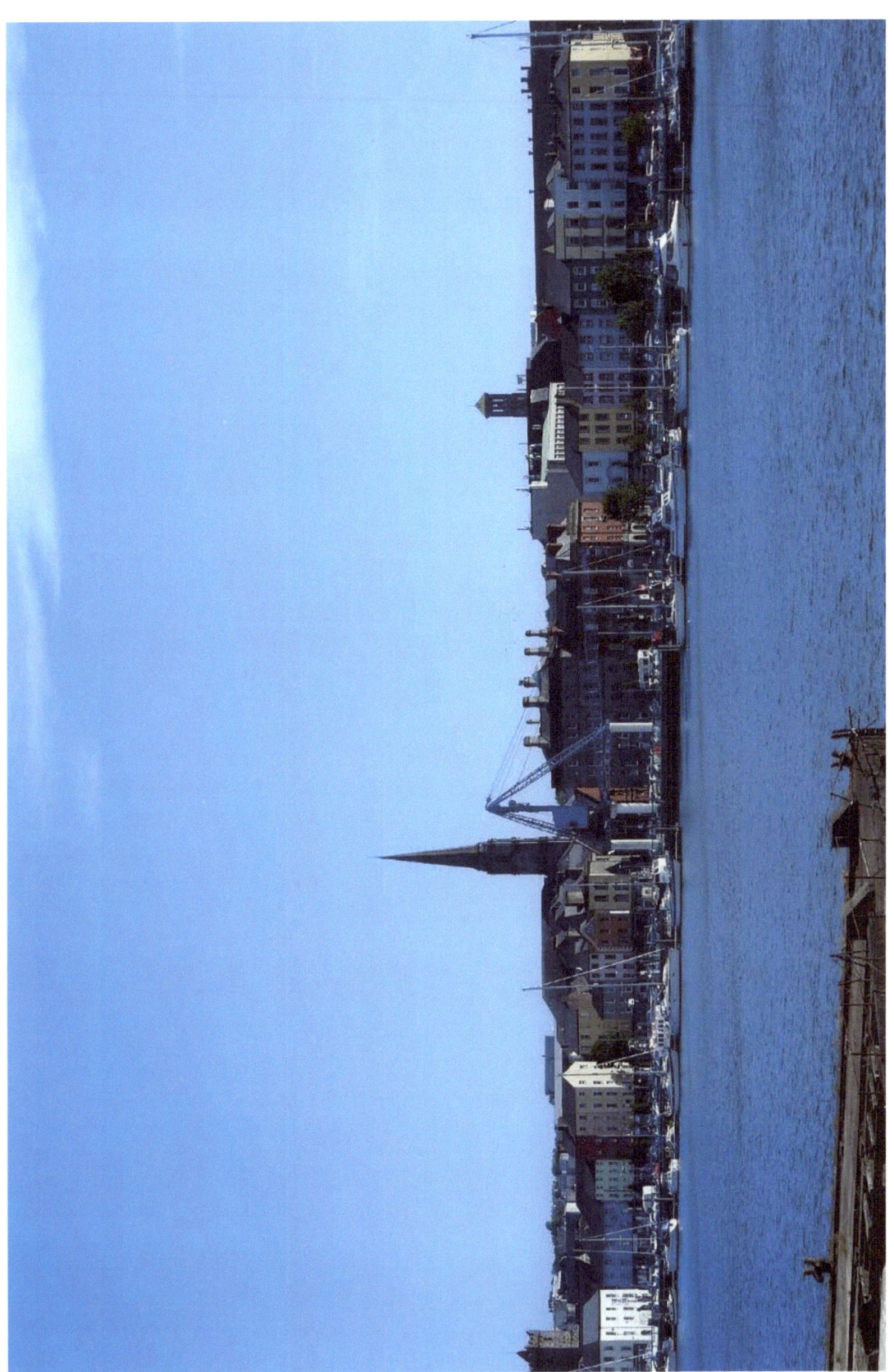

Waterford –The Untaken City

Opposite: After a heavy rain shower in May, the sky was transformed with a large rainbow spanning the breathe of the River Suir.

Below: The Star Pride pictured at evening time heading down River from Waterford City. A German built ship with a passenger capacity of up to 208. On December 22, 2015, the Star Pride hit a reef near the pacific coast of Panama. The passengers and crew were stranded for over 15 hours on Coiba, a Panamanian island and national park. The passengers were rescued by another Windstar boat, the Star Breeze, and Paul Gauguin's ship, the Tere Moana. She was salvaged and put back into service on June 9, 2016.

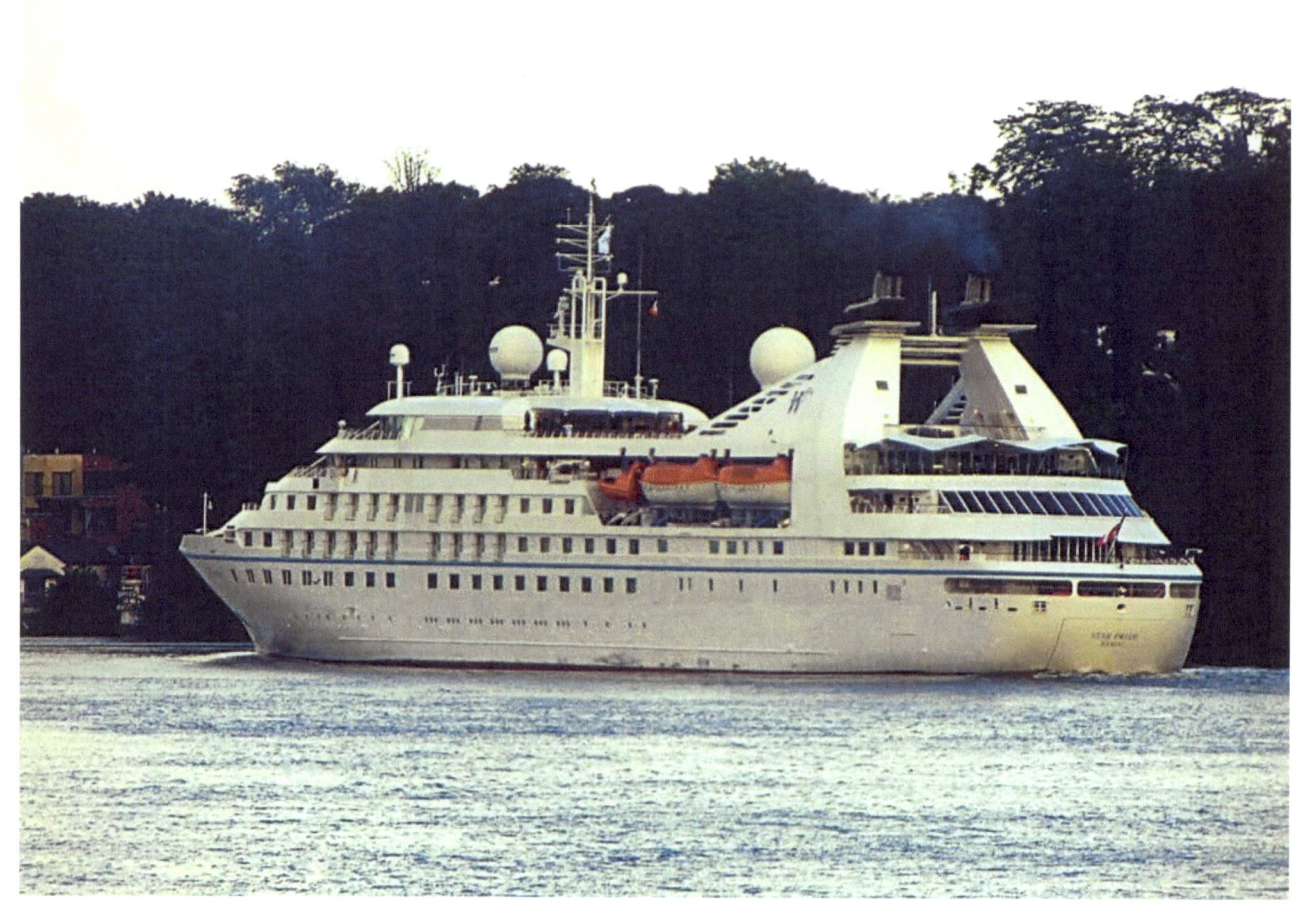

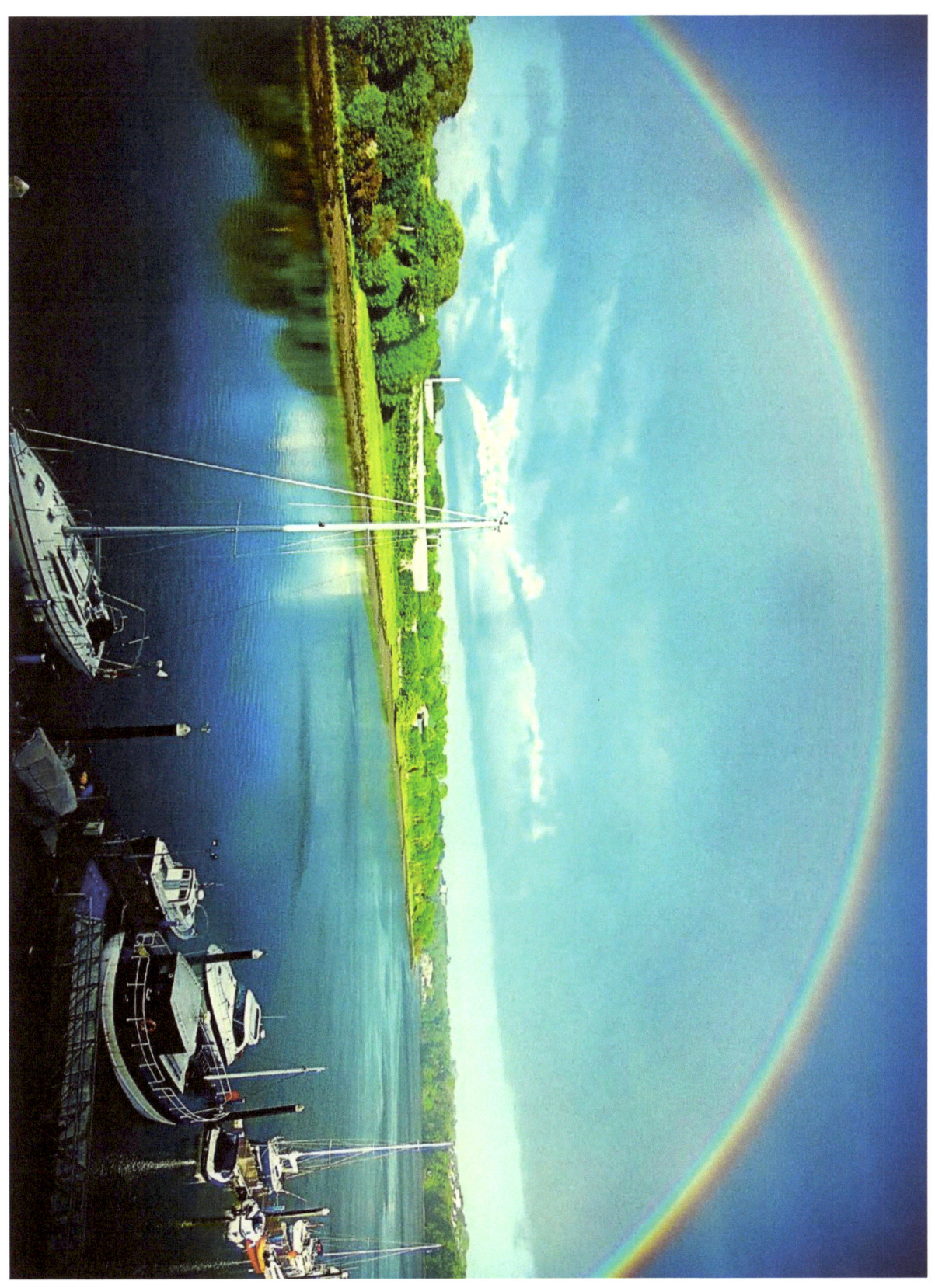

Below: The ruins of Greyfriar's. In 1241 King Henry III agreed to the building of a Franciscan Friary here.

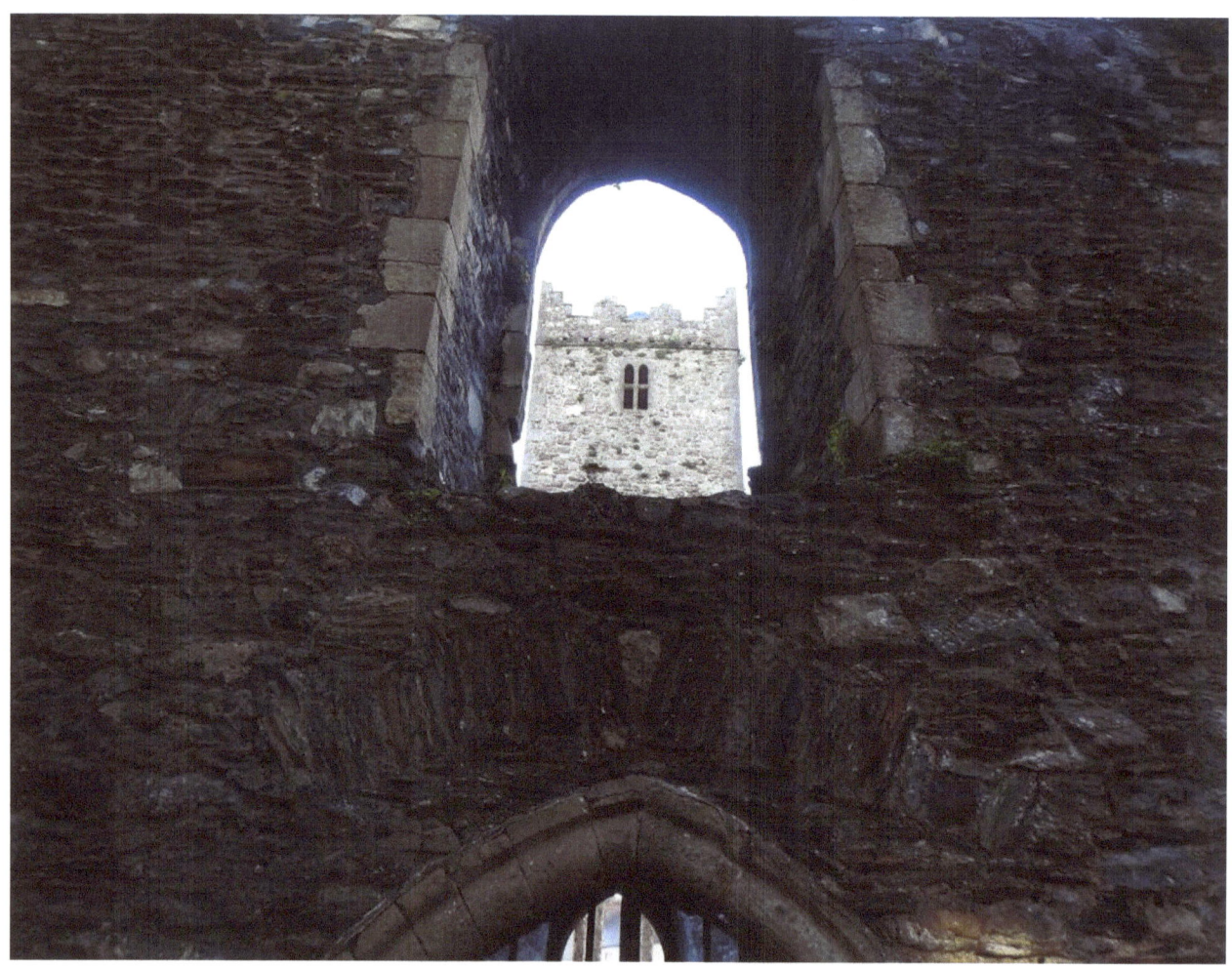

Below: The statue of Luke Wadding stands outside the Old Franciscan Friary on Greyfriar's Street.

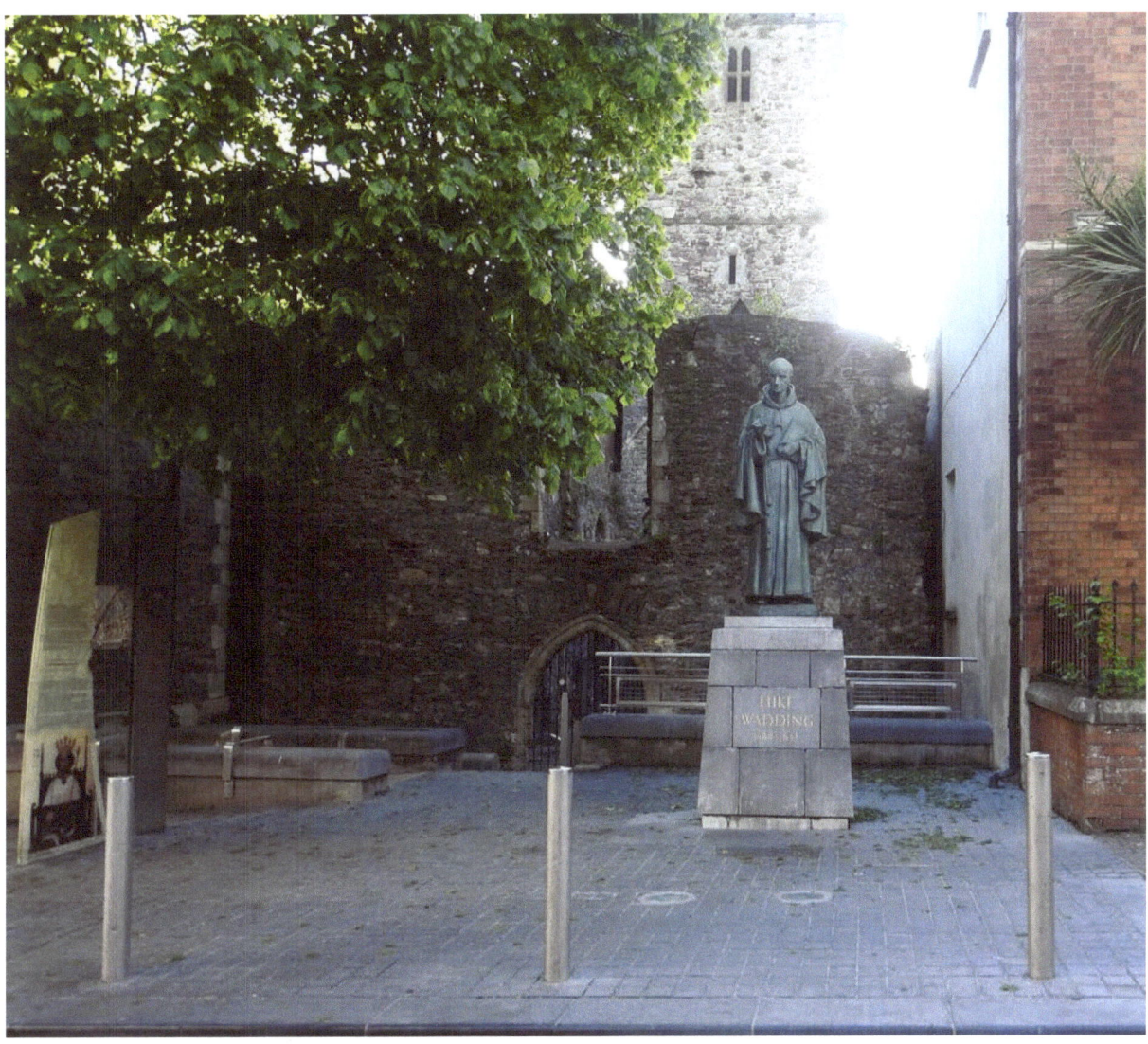

Below: A lesser black-backed gull seen on the River close to the city. Waterford city is a relatively short distance from the coast and hence is host to birds more often seen at the sea-side.

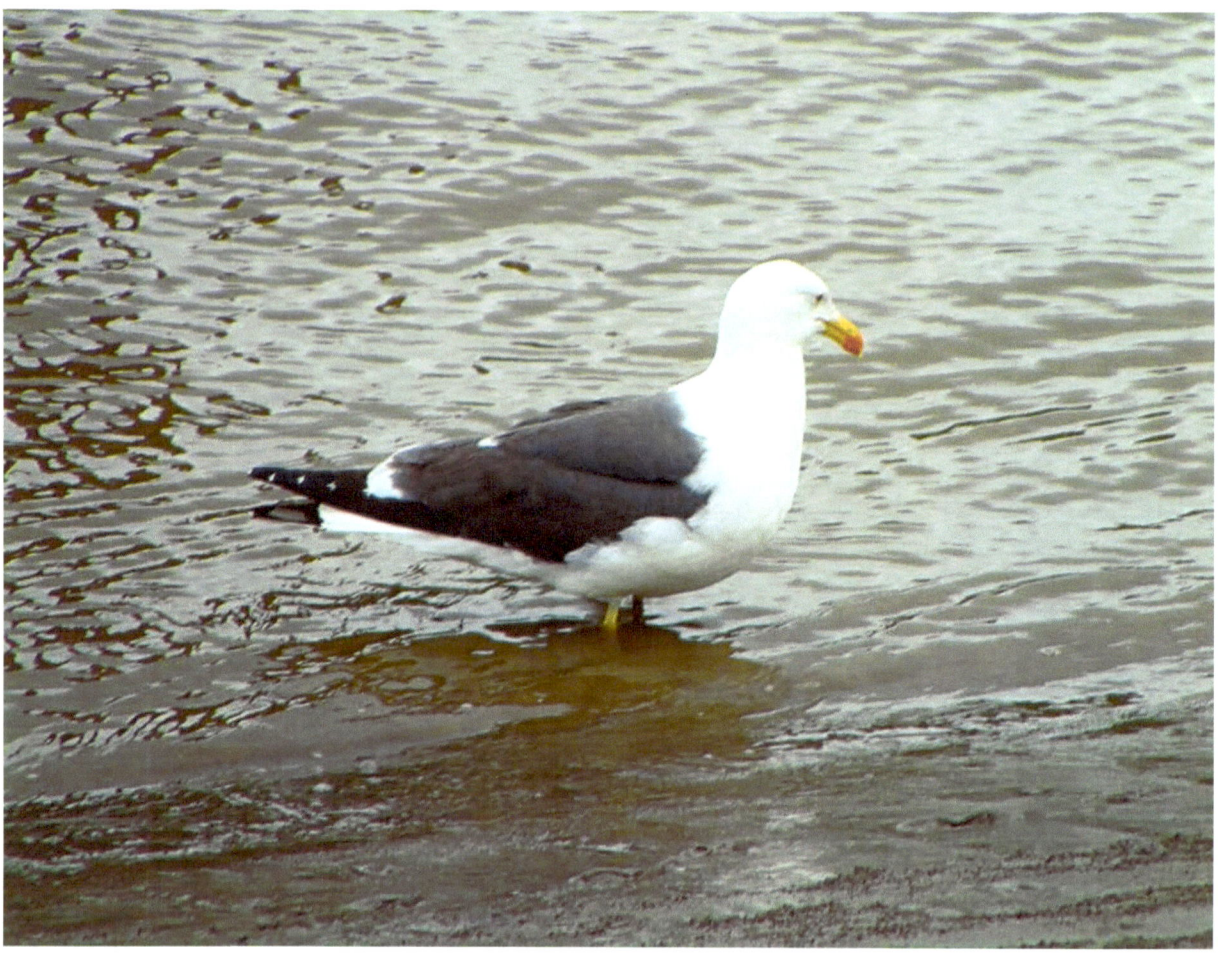

Bye-Laws of Waterford City from The Great Parchment Book of Waterford (Liber Antiquissimus Civitatis Waterfordiae)

1382: It was ordained that all hogs, boars and all other swine and pigs that should be found by day or by night walking within the said City or in the trenches and dykes that they shall be slain and killed.

1473: It was ordained that who so ever man or woman have swine walking in the City or Suburbs if they walk within the city or break men's gardens or parks or do any hurt that they be slain.

1475: It was ordained and enacted that no manner of man, woman nor child put no manner of dung, ramell or filth into the River over no quay nor slip of the City.

1484: It was enacted that what so ever person or persons, man, woman or child break or perish any glass window or windows...of any Church or Chapel within the City or Suburbs...it be lawful to levy 6s. 8d. Of such person or persons...and if he be a child of none age that the action may be conceived...against the father or mother.

1578: To have the time known for servants to rise, workmen and artificers to begin and attend their labour, it was ordered that at five of the clock in the morning at all seasons of the year the great bell in the cathedral church should be rung by the Sexton.

Quotes on the History of the People's Park

"As the oozy marsh and swamp has made way for the smooth lawn and green clump...so I trust the reeking public house and the hateful whiskey shop will be widely exchanged for the pure breeze of heaven, the quiet repose of feeble age and the healthful gambols of rejoicing youth."

George Howard, 7th Earl of Carlisle, Lord Lieutenant of Ireland, at the official opening of the People's Park, August, 1857

...waste and weary swamp covered with dank and fetid water, exhaling noxious vapours by night, and by day presenting a picture of hapless wretchedness which was a derision and disgrace to us...aided by the hand of man, flings forth from its generous breast, verdure and bloom and beauty to cheer the eye and gladden the hearts of all who visit there.

Waterford Chronicle, 7th of February, 1857

Quotes on the History of the River Suir

The Mall is a beautiful walk, about 200 yards long and proportionately broad. The draining and levelling the ground which was formerly marsh was done at a very considerable expence; it is planted with rows of Elms. Here the Ladies and Gentlemen assemble on fine evenings where they have the opportunity of each other's conversation. Nothing can be more agreeable than to see this shady walk crowded with the fair sex of the city taking the air, enjoying the charms of a pleasant evening and improving their healths; this city is celebrated for the beauties of its female inhabitants. Near the Mall is a pleasant Bowling-green...which makes this part of the town (affording the prospect of the river and shipping) very agreeable.

Charles Smith, 1746

The finest object in this city is the Quay, unrivalled by any I have seen, an English mile long, the great river Suir is near a mile over, flows up to the town in one noble reach and the opposite shore a bold hill which rises from the water to a height that renders the whole magnificent.

Arthur Young, 1780

Contact the author:

mywaterford@gmail.com

www.ingramcontent.com/pod-product-compliance
Lightning Source LLC
Chambersburg PA
CBHW041315180526
45172CB00004B/1110